Concorde
The Inside Story

Brian Trubshaw

Foreword by Captain Jock Lowe Ph.D., B.Sc. (hons), FRAes

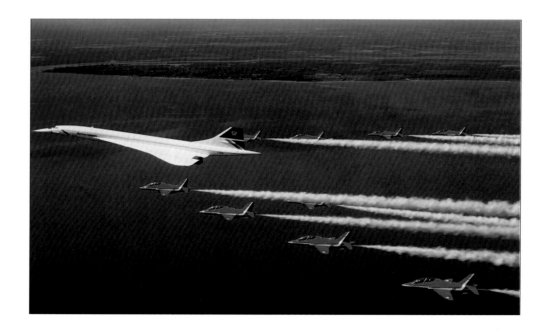

SUTTON PUBLISHING

First published in 2000 by
Sutton Publishing Limited · Phoenix Mill
Thrupp · Stroud · Gloucestershire · GL5 2BU

This new revised edition first published in 2001

Reprinted in 2002

British Library Cataloguing in Publication Data
A catalogue record for this book is available from the British Library

ISBN 0 7509 2811 5

Title page: *Hawk jets of the RAF's Red Arrows aerobatic display team tuck in close behind
Concorde 'Alpha-Alpha' over the south coast of England on the run-in to London-
Heathrow, to commemorate the airport's fiftieth anniversary, 2 June 1999. (BAe Systems)*

Concorde turn around at Melbourne during route proving, August 1975. (BAe Systems)

Typeset in 10/13pt Sabon.
Typesetting and origination by
Sutton Publishing Limited.
Printed in Great Britain by
J.H. Haynes & Co. Ltd, Sparkford

CONTENTS

High flight: with a dramatic cloudscape spread beneath them, four Concordes are captured by the photographer's lens in loose formation over southern England. (BAe Systems)

FOREWORD

CAPTAIN JOCK LOWE, PH.D., B.SC. (HONS), FRAES

The opportunity to make a significant technological advance happens only rarely. It is important that when it does occur, the chance is not missed. Yet so often the difference between success and failure lies in the hands of a small number of men. Concorde was and still is an example.

In the case of Concorde there is no doubt, regardless of where the topic is debated, that Brian Trubshaw was one of these special people. His drive, energy and enthusiasm, coupled with his ability to lead and organise were first class. To be present at one of his post-flight debriefing sessions, to see the respect awarded him by the assembled pilots, engineers and scientists, was a perfect example of these attributes being recognised by all.

Brian has been working with Concorde for more than thirty years. His knowledge of the Concorde project is second to none. I am delighted that he can put some of his memories into this book so that we can all share the highs and lows which have always accompanied this beautiful aircraft. The honour I feel to have to write this foreword will, I am sure, be matched by your enjoyment as you read it.

ACKNOWLEDGEMENTS

I am very grateful to Jonathan Falconer of Sutton Publishing for encouraging me to write this book, as my natural inclination was a feeling that there were already sufficient books written on Concorde.

My step-daughter, Sally Edmondson, has been a tower of strength in helping me as well as typing out the full manuscript and I am eternally grateful to her.

British Aerospace has been most supportive and my thanks are due to Howard Berry and Shaun Greene and David Charlton of British Aerospace Airbus for all their help and permission to use photographs and charts. Shaun Greene lent me copies of *Concorde News*, which have been most useful in recalling so much of what went on. Dr Norman Barfield, who has now retired from British Aerospace, has once again given me much help and reminders. And then there is John Dickens to thank for all his help in lending me material and recalling large parts of the Concorde programme.

From British Airways, nothing has been too much trouble. Captain Jock Lowe and Captain Mike Bannister have been a tremendous help and source of information. I say thank you to Kate Gay and Bill Fernandez for producing photographic material and confirming permission to use it. As well as to Captain David Leney. And last but not least to Rolls-Royce Heritage and to the Concorde Engine Support Organisation.

Many photographs have been supplied by Peter R. March from his unique collection, for which I am extremely grateful. I also thank Adrian Meredith for coming to an agreement that enabled me to use a photograph showing the inside of the Concorde simulator at Filton, and to Christopher Orlebar for the use of some of his Concorde slides.

In November 1998 I was fortunate to be asked to participate in a Witness Seminar on Concorde arranged by the Institute of Contemporary British History and organised by Dr Peter Catterrall, Executive Director of ICBH. This historic occasion was divided into three sessions covering policy, technology and flight operations. This was the best memory jogger imaginable. The participants were:

Session 1
Peter Jay (Chairman), Sir Peter Baldwin, Christopher Benjamin, Handel Davies, Etienne Fage, Nick Gardner, Lord Jenkins of Hillhead, Sir Philip Jones, Eric Lewis and M.C. Neale.

Session 2
Captain Jock Lowe (Chairman), Frank Armstrong, G.H.S. Barton, Peter Champion, Dudley Collard, Professor Fowes Williams, John Hutchinson,

Concorde 002, with the author at the controls, overflies Buckingham Palace, 14 June 1969. (Author)

Rt. Hon. Aubrey Jones, Simon Aubrey Jones, Jean Rech, S.J. Swadling and myself.

Session 3
Sir Neil Collons (Chairman), Peter Baker, Richard Beckett, Ken Binning, Rt. Hon. Edmund Dell, Mrs Eileen Denza, Derek John, John McEnery, Henri Perrier, Guy Thornton Smith and Brian Walpole.

I understand that Kenneth Owen is compiling a manuscript covering these proceedings and in due course this will become recorded history.

There are a numerous names that could have been mentioned but this has not been possible. Nevertheless, I give my most sincere thanks to all who have designed Concorde, tested it on the ground and in the air, built it, inspected it for flight, maintained it and operated it and all the other supporting services both technical, operational and administrative.

I am also grateful for the personal contact that I have had with Sir James Hamilton and Sir Philip Jones.

PROLOGUE

Concorde 002 was parked on the southern turning circle of the NE/SW runway at Filton, quite near the threshold of Runway 28, which had to be used because of the crash barrier at the western end. At Z minus 2 hours the detailed operational plan was cranked into action. This included closing the A38 Gloucester Road that runs past the boundary of Filton airfield prior to take-off, and the closure of RAF Fairford to all other air traffic. Crew safety equipment to be worn was specified in the following order: protective helmets, low-altitude equipment and Air Ventilated Suit (AVS) together with parachute.

The crew for 002 consisted of: Brian Trubshaw – Captain; John Cochrane – Co-pilot; Brian Watts – Flight Engineer; John Allan – Senior Flight Test Engineer; Mike Addley – Flight Test Observer; and Peter Holding – Flight Test Observer.

002 takes off on her maiden flight from Filton to Fairford on 9 April 1969. Fairford was chosen as the test airfield for Concorde because the runway at Filton was not long enough for protoype test flying. (BAe Systems)

We were driven out to 002 from the Flight Operations building in order to commence the very lengthy and protracted pre-flight checklist, which lasted for more than one hour before engine start was requested. A few more checks followed engine start before John Cochrane requested taxi clearance, it being our normal practice for the co-pilot to operate the radio communication with Air Traffic Control (ATC). The short taxi to Runway 28 and the pre-take-off checks were now complete. John Cochrane then requested take-off clearance, which was given by Roy Julian, SATCO, Filton, who finished with the words '. . . and good luck gentlemen'.

I then selected full thrust against the wheel brakes, which blasted the hell out of the A38 and selected reheat 'on'. No. 3 reheat did not light the first time, but a second attempt was successful. With that I released the brakes and we were off down the runway with an extremely rapid acceleration. The chase plane, a Canberra flown by Johnnie Walker, formated on the right side as 002 rolled down the runway. In case of any problems, a HS125 was also on standby as a back-up chase.

100 knots (k) came, no flag and on we went, rotating at 140k to a pitch attitude of about 15°. Lift off occurred at about 180k and was

The author with John Cochrane, the co-pilot, on the flightdeck of 002 at Fairford in 1969. (BAe Systems)

increased to 220k by 1,000ft where a gentle right-hand turn towards Fairford was initiated. The landing gear and nose/visor was left down for the whole flight.

After the drama of take-off there was little conversation among the crew, so I thought that I had better say a few words to the effect that everything felt fine and that we were doing very well. On this maiden flight I carried out general handling checks and assessed the use of auto-throttle and engine responses en route, up to 280k and a height of 8,000ft.

Brize Norton radar positioned 002 for a final approach of 10nm flown at 170k, but on turning on to finals both radio altimeters failed. This was decidedly unfriendly as their use was (and is) standard procedure to assist in judging the last 100 feet or so before touchdown. In the case of Concorde it is especially crucial because the pilot's line of sight is some 38 feet above the ground when the main wheels touch due to the aircraft's nose-high attitude. The first landing, therefore, had to be eye-balled resulting in an arrival, which was not too bad, about ½ a second early. Immediately after touchdown I selected reverse thrust and the braking parachute was streamed. A short taxi to the running base in the south-west corner of Fairford airfield, where a VIP reception party awaited, terminated this epic flight of 22 minutes flight time and 43 minutes block time.

The whole crew were thrilled and felt a great sense of achievement, although they realised this was only the beginning of a long journey. The rest of the day was spent de-briefing at Fairford, before flying back to Filton to consume some of 002's birthday cake, which had been made specially by the famous and brave lady aviator, the late Sheila Scott, and to receive gifts from the other directors. The evening was spent in the 'local' with all those who had put 002 together and cleared her for flight.

Concorde 002 touching down on its maiden flight at RAF Fairford escorted by the chase Canberra, 9 April 1969. (BAe Systems)

Concorde crossing the airfield boundary at RAF Fairford for the first time with resident RAF Hercules C130 transports in the background, 9 April 1969. (BAe Systems)

INTRODUCTION

It is not unreasonable to look upon Concorde as a miracle. Who would have predicted that the combination of two governments, two airframe companies, two engine companies – each with different cultures, languages and units of measurement – would have produced a technical achievement the size of Concorde? Sir George Edwards, Chairman of the British Aircraft Corporation, once remarked that: 'These are not usually taken to be the ingredients of success . . . These international programmes tried men's very souls.'

When it started, Concorde was itself an ambitious project to say the least. There was no precedent for a major international supersonic civil project surrounded, not surprisingly, by national pride.

Sir George Edwards, Chairman of the British Aircraft Corporation, without whom Concorde would not have happened, with the author and author's wife, Yvonne, at Sir George's retirement reception at Weybridge, c. 1976. (BAe Systems)

André Turcat, Director of Flight Test at Sud Aviation who flew 001 on its maiden flight in 1969, with Neil Armstrong of NASA, the first man on the moon, and the author at the Society of Experimental Test Pilots Symposium in Los Angeles, c. 1972. (Author)

But let no one underestimate the magnitude of the task that the Concorde project represented. This one fact has never been emphasised or understood as much as it should have been. History will no doubt debate the whys and wherefores of doing the programme in the first place, but it happened in spite of everything and now Concorde flies daily across the Atlantic, in the main from London and Paris to New York and back, like clockwork. This achievement is hailed as marvellous by many people, an attitude that would have been very helpful in the early stages. Many challenges and difficulties needed to be overcome in order to make the Concorde programme happen. There is probably no single person who will ever know of all the grief and woe, frustrations, difficulties and disappointments that have been prevailed over.

On 5 August 1966, a second meeting with Sir George Edwards changed my life. This was the occasion when I was appointed as Chief Test Pilot of the Concorde project on the British side. To have been involved with Concorde for over twenty years, with a diminished but close relationship with British Airways and the Concorde fleet for another fifteen, is the highlight of my aviation career. Luck was certainly on my side when I was appointed following an official complaint from the Airworthiness Review Board regarding British test-pilot input. I was proud then and proud now to have been so intimately involved, but that is not to say that I did not suffer any misgivings as we all fought our way through the wrangling and frustrations.

Many books have been written about Concorde, some of which are very good and these include: Kenneth Owen's *Concorde – New Shape in the Sky*; Chris Orlebar's *The Concorde Story*; Brian Calvert's *Flying Concorde*, many others are disappointing. I have tried to make this book different because of my unique position in the Concorde story, highlighting some aspects that generally have not been aired before. It is my view of the evolution of Concorde through enormous periods of turmoil while strenuous efforts were made, mainly by Government, to cancel the project.

BAC's own position could have been different if the BAC 3-11 project, a twin-engined transport similar in many ways to the Airbus A300, had survived – and the Position of 'UK Limited' as a plane builder for the world market might well have been very different to what it is today. I believe that BAC realised that the 3-11 would be a much better commercial proposition than Concorde was ever likely to be in terms of world sales. One only has to see the achievements of Airbus today to appreciate the wisdom behind their thinking. I have always been intrigued that Bernard Ziegler, son of General Henri Ziegler, President of Aérospatiale, left the French Air Force Flight Test Centre where he was a test pilot and went to the A300 programme, not the Concorde. Bernard Ziegler went from being a test pilot to Director of Flight Test and Director of Engineering at Airbus while still maintaining his test-pilot role. His contribution to the success of the Airbus projects is mammoth and quite rightly he has received many accolades.

In order to understand the concept of Concorde, the western world's only successful supersonic commercial transport, it is necessary first to dwell on some of the background to supersonic flight, albeit from research and military aircraft experience. The flight regime for Concorde required special attention to every aspect of aircraft design, use of materials, airworthiness aspects, flight-test methods and procedures. In fact, the flight-development task and the time it took was greater than anything that had hitherto occurred in the civil transport field. In a project of such complexity some mistakes were inevitable, but it is a great credit to the design teams and others involved that serious in-flight dramas were so few. The various unique features of Concorde are described in some detail.

The way Concorde was sold to the world airlines is also reviewed. One needs to remember that when the Concorde programme started there were no firm orders and options/orders followed later. Normally, aircraft manufacturers launch a new project when they have acquired sufficient evidence to show that a minimum order of so many aircraft can be assumed with a reasonable degree of certainty. Concorde did not follow this pattern and it will be seen how this resulted in many changes when the airlines did become involved. Compare this to the Boeing 747 project where Pan-American World Airways, then in its heyday, played a vital part in the concept and initial order.

The story of how much Concorde cost to develop and build will live forever, one way or another. However, not every fact that is shouted from

The author in front of Concorde 002 at RAF Fairford, 1972. (BAe Systems)

The part played by British Airways has been central to the Concorde success story. Pictured on the stand at London-Heathrow's Terminal 4 in December 1989, is BA's 'Alpha-Alpha'. (Jonathan Falconer)

the rooftops is necessarily true. The information that I provide here is intended to give an accurate and fair picture. I also take a look at the part played by British Airways, a point of particular interest because the 'unwilling bride' has been transformed into the champion of Concorde, while Air France has followed a more subdued pattern in later years.

I hope that readers will enjoy the chapters that follow. It is difficult not to get technical in some places, and while this may please the aviation enthusiast, it may not appeal to the lay person, but you cannot win them all!

Brian Trubshaw
January 2000

THE START OF SUPERSONIC FLIGHT

The term often used to describe flight very close to the speed of sound is the 'sound barrier', but while this implies something exciting, it is really quite meaningless because there is no sound barrier. As an aircraft flies, it disturbs the air around it that forms into little molecules of pressure which in turn expand at the speed of sound. The closer an aircraft flies to the speed of sound, the less time there is for these molecules to literally 'get out of the way' in any direction. It is easiest to visualise this phenomenon as the bow wave of a ship or boat. There is no problem at subsonic speeds, but as the speed of sound is approached these pressure waves form into a build-up in front of the aircraft to produce an invisible cone. At the speed of sound (Mach=1.0) the cone changes into a flat shockwave which can be regarded as an invisible wall, hence the term 'sound barrier'. Beyond the speed of sound, the shock waves revert to a conical shape. A similar wave from the tail behaves in much the same way as the air expands back to normal pressure. The effect of breaking the sound barrier depends on whether the aircraft was designed for supersonic speeds in the first place, but like most advances in aviation the knowledge that is now available was not gained without very high risks, catastrophies and loss of life.

It is the passage of an aircraft through the speed of sound that results in the sonic boom that can be heard on the ground all the time that the aircraft is supersonic. Some believe that the boom only occurs as M=1.0 is passed, but if you could run as fast as the aircraft you would hear a boom all the time creating a sort of carpet. The highest intensity of over-pressure is immediately beneath the aircraft.

Supersonic flight brings with it a set of problems not usually experienced in subsonic flight, of

The boom reaches the ground as a carpet which is at maximum intensity immediately below the aircraft. Concorde also produces a secondary boom of much lower intensity, which is often heard in the south of England depending on weather conditions. (BAe Systems)

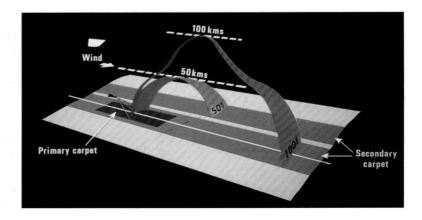

which control difficulties are the most obvious. Even the first aircraft that were designed for supersonic flight experienced many control problems in what is best described as the transonic region of the flight envelope, i.e. the regime between subsonic and supersonic flight.

An example of this problem is the North American F.100 which could fly supersonic in straight and level flight and was the first of the 'Century' series of American jet fighters. Several military test pilots were not entirely happy with some of its flight characteristics but were accused of nit-picking by the constructor, North American, which persuaded the US Air Force that the deficiencies in the F100 were in the extreme corner of the flight envelope and would be unlikely to cause pilot problems. The Chairman of North American, Dutch Kindelberger, won the battle but lost the war. After about 200 F100s had been delivered in 1954, Wheaties Welch, the Chief Test Pilot of North American, was killed diving an F100 at M=1.4. The aircraft disintegrated but the flight recorders showed that it was directionally unstable. All the F100s went back to the manufacturers for modification, which included a larger tail and a new flight-control system.

However, investigations into the problems associated with supersonic flight were carried out during the 1940s using, first, high-performance piston-engined fighters like the Supermarine Spitfire and then later with the initial batch of jet-engined aircraft. Because this work was carried out during the Second World War, it was cloaked in secrecy. Many will wonder why such high-risk flights were made in the first place and what is the magic of speed. As will be noted in the next chapter, aviation, and

Bell X-I in which Captain Charles 'Chuck' Yeager of the US Air Force exceeded Mach 1 (M=1.0) for the first time reaching M=1.06 in level flight on 14 October 1947. (P. March)

especially civil transport, is all about speed. Many of the Second World War fighter pilots had experienced strange and indeed unpleasant flight characteristics when diving at speeds close to the speed of sound, when the flight controls were seen to do the opposite to what was expected of them. There was also noticeable airframe buffet which became very severe on some aircraft types, almost to the point of structural break-up. It was important to keep ahead of Germany in this field and similar work was going on in the USA.

Consequently, RAE Farnborough planned a programme of high-speed dives using a Spitfire PRXI (photo-reconnaissance version) with a Merlin 70 engine. In order to achieve the greatest possible dive speed, it was necessary to climb to as high an altitude as possible – in the Spitfire tests, the aircraft was climbed to 40,000ft. In 1943, Squadron Leader Martindale of Aero Flight (and who later became a test pilot at Rolls-Royce) commenced such a dive of about 45° and in just over 30 seconds he attained a speed of M=0.9 at 29,000ft descending. During the course of the dive he experienced the aircraft displaying a strong tendency to pitch nose down along with increased drag, loss of lift and buffeting. It is possible that this flight came very close to exceeding the speed of sound. Some years later I remember Squadron Leader Martindale giving a lecture at the Royal Air Force Flying College, Manby, when I was a member of the staff and I regarded him with some awe.

The Douglas X-3 Sky Rocket was the first aircraft to reach M=2.0, flown by Scott Crossfield at NACA (NASA) in November 1953. Originally it was flown by Bill Bridgeman of Douglas, who described it as a little beast. (P. March)

The Fairey Delta 2 (right) in formation with the other Fairey Delta modified with a Concorde-type ogee wing to become the BAC221. (BAe Systems)

The advent of jet fighters gave further input to these investigations world wide. However, apart from confirming the obvious problem areas, few did any better than the Spitfire – if as good. Some of the jet-engined -powered fighter/research aircraft had the benefit of swept wings, which were considered to offer major advantages for supersonic flight because the increase in drag when flying near Mach 1.0 was delayed. The German Messerschmitt Me 163 Komet was configured in this manner without a tail, resulting in an interceptor capable of very high speeds over a short period thanks largely to its rocket engine. Much of the development flying on the Me 163 was carried out by the famous lady test pilot Hanna Reitsch, whose presentation to the Society of Experimental Test Pilots many years later resulted in a standing ovation lasting several minutes.

Britain's entry into the jet age was marked with the first flight of the Gloster E28/39 by Gerry Sayer on 15 May 1941 from RAF Cranwell, as Gloster's airfield at Brockworth on the outskirts of Gloucester was unsuitable. The flight lasted 17 minutes.

In 1943 the British Government issued specification E24/43 for an experimental transonic aircraft intended to reach speeds of 1,000 mph at 36,000ft (M=1.5). This resulted in the Miles M.52 design, a single-engine aircraft with a bullet-shaped cylindrical fuselage and a jettisonable nose section containing a pressurised cockpit for the pilot. By 1946, it was 90 per cent complete but was cancelled in favour of air-launched models powered by liquid-fuel rocket motors and released from Mosquito aircraft at 40,000ft. The E24/43 (Miles M-52) was to use a Frank Whittle-designed engine, the Power Jets W2/700.

The USA took the lead in supersonic flight experience when Captain Charles 'Chuck' Yeager of the US Air Force reached M=1.06 in level flight in the Bell X-1 on 14 October 1947, a rocket-powered and air-launched research aircraft. This task would normally have been carried out by Bell's test pilot, Slick Goodlin, who had contracted to fly it to M=0.8, which he did. This was Phase 1. He then renegotiated his contract and demanded $150,000 to go beyond M1=0. Phase 2 was to take the Bell X-1 to M=1.1. Seemingly, Slick Goodlin's wishes for method of payment resulted in a prolonged argument between the company, its lawyers and Slick himself. The Chief Test Pilot of Bell, Tex Johnston, with whom I met up with when he was Director of Flight Test at Boeing, Seattle, did one flight up to M=0.75 to verify the dangers involved. In the meantime the US Air Force became disenchanted with all these wrangles and consequently decided to use an Air Force test pilot to continue the programme. Much to his own surprise Chuck Yeager was selected, having been interviewed by Colonel Al Boyd (later to become General Boyd and who approved my flights in the USAF B58 supersonic bomber). Al Boyd acquainted Chuck Yeager with the high level of risk involved in extending flight into the unknown.

The X-1 did not take off in the conventional sense but was dropped from a B-29 Superfortress bomber mother ship at about 25,000ft like a bomb. This gave the pilot time to jettison fuel and carry out a dead-stick (i.e. without engine) landing on the lake bed at Edwards Air Force Base, California, from where the flights took place. It is my belief that this unique facility at Edwards played a major role in the way that American military and research aircraft were developed.

The Bell X-2 followed and then came the Douglas X-3 D558-2 Skyrocket, which became the first aircraft to fly at M=2.0. It was flown by a Douglas test pilot, Bill Bridgeman who was a former Navy fighter pilot. Bill achieved M=1.8 and Scott Crossfield a civilian test pilot at NACA (later to become NASA) was the first to break M=2.0. There were many hairy moments in these aircraft from which there was no escape – the canopy was literally bolted down. This was accepted on the premiss that survival from a jump out at such speeds and altitude was impossible. Nevertheless, some of the pilots expressed a 'naked' feeling when stepping into an experimental aircraft with no exit. After the first flight of the X-3 in February 1948, Bill Bridgeman was asked the normal question of what he thought of it. 'It is a little beast!' was his reply.

Britain's first aircraft to exceed M=1.0 was the de Havilland DH108 Swallow which was evolved from the de Havilland Vampire to test stability and new control theories using swept-back wings with elevons, but without a tail. The first flight of the DH108 was made by de Havilland Chief Test Pilot Geoffrey de Havilland in May 1946. Geoffrey undertook all the initial flights until he was killed in the second DH108 on 27 September 1946 over the Thames Estuary, exploring the transonic threshold. His father wrote:

Geoffrey felt pretty certain that the machine had a chance of breaking the world speed record, which then stood at 616mph. It was arranged that he should try for the record in a few days' time and I saw him off

Britain's first aircraft to exceed M=1.0 was the de Havilland DH108. Geoffrey de Havilland carried out all the initial flying on the DH108 but was killed in the second DH108 on 27 September 1946. (P. March)

on a final test flight from Hatfield on the evening of September 27th. I was rung up at home in the evening with the news that he was long overdue, and that an aeroplane was reported to have exploded over the Thames Estuary. I dreaded the worst. At low tide next day wreckage was reported on the mud flats near Egypt Bay, just north of the village of Cliffe and north-east of Gravesend. Geoffrey's body was not found for several days and then much further down the river.

Geoffrey de Havilland, senior, had already lost another son, John, in an air collision between two Mosquito aircraft. John Cunningham, famous for his wartime achievements and from his work on many de Havilland products, including the worlds' first jet transport, the Comet, took over from Geoffrey de Havilland as Chief Test Pilot and inherited the DH108 programme as well as everything else. He soon found it necessary to employ another pair of hands and he chose Squadron Leader John Derry who was at Vickers Supermarine at the time but without much work to employ his talents. John Derry became the first pilot to exceed M=1.0 in a British-built aircraft, the DH108, diving from 40,000ft to about 25,000ft as the aircraft had insufficient engine power to achieve this speed in level flight.

John Derry's brilliant career, along with that of his flight test observer, Tony Richards, came to an abrupt end at the Farnborough Air Display on 6 September 1952 when the de Havilland DH110 (later the Sea Vixen) that he was demonstrating at speeds very close to M=1.0 broke up following structural failure caused by wing flutter. Its two engines continued on and crashed into the crowd, killing twenty-eight people and injuring sixty others seriously. I witnessed this tragedy with John Derry's wife, Eve, and John Cunningham from the pilot's enclosure. The flying show had to continue as quickly as practicable in order to keep the spectators as calm as possible. This brave lady stayed with us for a long time until John Cunningham took her away very quietly. So once again progress was achieved at a very high price. The DH108 flown by both John Cunningham and John Derry was handed over to Aero Flight RAE. Two commanding officers, Squadron Leaders Stuart Muller-Rowland and Eric Genders were killed in DH108 accidents, but when Genders was killed on 1 May 1950 at Hartley Witney the saga of this experimental aircraft came to an end. Before this some fifty-one flights were made by Chris Capper, who had joined Aero Flight in 1949 and later moved to de Havilland as a civilian test pilot.

In the USA the 'Century' series fighters followed the F100 with the F101, F102, F104, F105, F106. Of these the F104 proved operational service at M=2.0. This aircraft incorporated a downward ejection escape system deemed to have been the reason for some of the fatalities in F104 accidents. One of the US Air Force's outstanding test pilots, Iven C. Kincheloe, died in a F104. His widow presented a highly coveted award in his name to the Society of Experimental Test Pilots, given annually for significant achievement in flight testing. In 1971 the award went to André Turcat and myself for Concorde. In 1956 Convair flew the B58 supersonic delta winged bomber which reached M=2.0, but not without major catastrophe in the course of its relatively short period of service. If the

Geoffrey de Havilland, junior, who lost his life in the DH108 when exploring the transonic threshold. (de Havilland photograph)

B58 supersonic bomber built by Convair for the US Air Force. The author was allocated 10 hours familiarisation flying with this aircraft at Edwards Air Force Base, California, in 1968. (Author)

The English Electric Lightning became the RAF's first operational fighter with sustained performance of M=2.0. The Lightning had a phenomenal rate of climb. (P. March)

auto-stabilisation system was not functioning and an outboard engine failure occurred, the fin came off.

Meanwhile, in Britain supersonic experience was gathering momentum when Roly Beamont, Chief Test Pilot of English Electric, a most-distinguished and highly decorated RAF fighter pilot on Typhoons and Tempests in the Second World War, flew the English Electric P1A, which exceeded M=1.0 on its third flight in 1954. The P1B followed and was the first British Aircraft to exceed M=2.0. The English Electric Lightning evolved from the P1A and P1B and became Britain's first operational fighter with sustained performance of M=2.0. The Lightning had an outstanding rate of climb, as good if not better than some present-day fighters. The Lightning was well established in squadron service by 1960 and carried out many interceptions on Russian bombers that infiltrated British air space. In later years Roly Beamont and myself were counterparts in the military aircraft divisions and in the commercial aircraft division respectively at British Aircraft Corporation.

On 10 March 1956 a Fairey Delta research aircraft flown by Peter Twiss, another well-known and respected name in the field of test flying, established a world speed record of 1,132mph along a route located on

Fairey Delta 2 flying with BAC221; FD2 has an ogee wing formation. WG774 held the world speed record of 1,132mph and the record-breaking flight was made by Peter Twiss in 1956. (BAe Systems)

Gerfaut 1A, which exceeded M=1.0 in level flight in about 1956. (P. March)

Trident I, flown by Jacques Guiguard, co-pilot of Concorde 001. Trident II reached 1,242mph in January 1957. (P. March)

the west side of France. Two FD2s were built and one of them was later modified with a Concorde-type ogee wing and became the BAC 221.

In France M=1.0 in level flight was exceeded by the Gerfaut 1A. The Sud-Ouest Aviation SO9000 Trident II followed and reached 1,242mph in January 1957. Jacques Guiguard, who flew as co-pilot on the first flight of Concorde 001, carried the scars of two major crashes in the Trident. In 1956 the SE212 Durandal reached M=1.5 on its maiden flight, while two more prototypes, the Mirage III and the Nord 1500 Griffon, exceeded M=2.0 in level flight. The Griffon was linked to Concorde because André Turcat, the first pilot of Concorde, established a world speed record of 1,018 mph over 100km closed circuit in 1959 and went on to reach M=2.19 (1,448 mph) at 15,240ft, thus becoming the first European to exceed M=2.0. Therefore, by the end of the 1950s the problems of supersonic flight from a technical standpoint were well known and flight at M=2.0 could be regarded as routine.

In this period, Bristol Aircraft (later part of British Aircraft Corporation) tendered successfully for an aircraft specified as ER134, the purpose of which was to study kinetic heating effects at a stagnation temperature of 250°C. This necessitated a speed of M=2.75 sustained for sufficient time to permit structural temperatures to stabilise. Light alloys were out of the question for meeting these requirements, so the use of stainless steel was adopted, although the metal chosen posed numerous problems with rigidity, strength, corrosion and weldability, as well as many others. By 1955, following close collaboration between Bristol and Firth Vickers, a layout was adopted. Originally, the Rolls-Royce engine that was to power the Avro supersonic bomber was selected, but the notorious White Paper

The Mirage III was capable of M=2.0 in level flight and was flown by all the Concorde lead test pilots, including the author. (BAe Systems)

Nord 1500 Griffon, which also exceeded M=2.0 in level flight. (P. March)

put forward by Duncan Sandys in 1957 cancelled the Avro project and also the advanced Saunders-Roe 177 mixed powerplant fighter. This left a number of de Havilland PS50 engines, developed from the Gyron Junior but with a reheat system and variable nozzle, available. The Government decreed that they be used for what was now called the Bristol 188.

Engine-surge problems in flight were major in the flight programmes of the two prototypes, both flown by Godfrey Auty in September 1962 and April 1963 respectively. A combination of inadequate duration and outmoded wing plan resulted in termination of the programme in 1964, by which time the maximum speed attained was M=1.88. The Bristol 188 highlighted many lessons and Sir George Edwards later commented that 'sometimes you have to spend money to learn how not to do it'.

For many of the years mentioned above, Dr Barnes Wallis was working on his moveable wing sweep, tailless Swallow project. He regarded configurations like Concorde as brute force and ignorance. A number of Swallow models were flown under remote control at Predannack in Cornwall, but Barnes Wallis would never agree to put a pilot into one of them following his very sincere feelings on the loss of life among the aircrews of 617 Squadron during the epic Ruhr Dams raid in May 1943. As a test pilot at Weybridge, I made frequent visits to meet Barnes Wallis, which were fascinating but failed to persuade him to change his mind. I did however notice that significant changes in design seemed to occur even more often than the actual visits. There is little doubt that the frequency of these modifications provided much ammunition for the opponents of his project. He also tended to brush aside details on how to seal the wing-sweep mechanism and used to say that he would leave it to the Dunlop Rubber Company. One envisaged a glorified condom flapping in the breeze.

THE CONCEPT OF CONCORDE

Aviation offers speed and speed is the very essence of air transportation. The advent of jet transports transformed journey times. Whereas aircraft like the Boeing Stratocruiser and the Lockheed Constellation took the best part of 12 hours to fly from London to New York, often with a stop at Shannon or Prestwick, the subsonic jets reduced this time to 7 or 8 hours. Claims used to be made that reducing journey times between major cities to within 12 hours increased trade.

The concept of Concorde was largely based on this time philosophy, offering as it does a quantum leap in speed as it cruises at twice the speed of sound (about 1,350mph) which is slightly faster than a rifle bullet, covering 20 nautical miles (nm) per minute. Now that speed is available, the air traveller's mind has turned towards cost and comfort, while in-flight entertainment has become big business. Airlines look towards economics with many new gimmicks to try and attract customers and so sell seats. The international civil aviation community is also very concerned about noise and other environmental issues.

In the mid-1950s, research and design studies into supersonic flight at the Royal Aircraft Establishment (RAE), and similar projects in France, undertook serious investigations. The formation in 1956 of the Supersonic Transport Advisory Committee (STAC) under Morien Morgan (Sir Morien Morgan), a deputy director of the RAE, was of particular significance. This committee was twenty-eight strong, including nine members from airframe manufacturers, four from engine companies, and the others from BOAC and BEA, all the leading research establishments, the Air Registration Board, Ministry of Transport and Civil Aviation and the Ministry of Supply. At this stage the rationalisation of the British airframe and aero-engine industry had not commenced. The STAC was supported by a thirty-eight-man technical sub-committee from the same organisations. Intensive research followed the STAC's first meeting on 5 November 1956 and some 400 written submissions were produced to prove that a civil supersonic transport was commercially viable. The work covered every aspect of aerodynamics including handling qualities, structures, systems, propulsion, economic and social impact (sonic boom and noise), the effect of kinetic heating, flight controls due to the movement of the wing's centre of pressure at supersonic speeds, vibrations and flutter and operational flexibility to function within the current environment, incorporating Air

Traffic Control. A long-range aircraft was the basis of the STAC's deliberations. Various configurations including M, W and Delta wing shapes were studied. The slender delta wing figured very prominently, as the others were only suitable for speeds lower than M=2.0.

It was recognised that the many new technical challenges of sustained supersonic flight required special attention. The first matter to decide was cruising speed. Close study of vehicle efficiency and taking account of the properties of structural materials when subjected to kinetic heating caused by skin friction from the air passing over it, all pointed to the choice of a cruising speed of about M=2.0. Adoption of speeds of M=2.6/2.7 soon lost favour because the STAC felt that the higher level of kinetic heating and the low-speed handling characteristics anticipated would result in high cost and longer development time. A great deal was known about military and research aircraft for speeds up to M=2.0, whereas knowledge of M=3.0 aircraft was virtually nil at the time. Experience of the Bristol 188 substantiated the Anglo-French views on the use of steel.

Britain was not alone in the consideration of supersonic transports (SST). Both French and American aircraft companies were extremely active in this field, not to mention what must have been happening in Russia behind closed doors. The original concept of Bristol was a six-engined Type 198. This configuration soon lost favour on technical grounds, especially weight, and re-emerged as the Bristol 223 with four engines.

Work in France was proceeding on similar lines to Britain except that Sud (later Aérospatiale) and their Design Director Pierre Satrè were convinced that a supersonic transport based on the Sud Caravelle, for ranges between 1,000–1,800 miles, was the answer for Air France to use on European and African routes. Clearly the impact of the sonic boom had not been thought through, but the French determination to have a medium-range version took a long time to die and was still part of the original Anglo-French Agreement when BAC and Sud teamed up to develop Concorde. The similarity between the British and French designs provoked considerable comment when shown in model form at the Paris Air Show in June 1961.

In the USA, Douglas, Boeing and Lockheed were all engaged in supersonic transport studies. I remember being introduced to the subject

Flight at supersonic speeds results in increased structural temperature due to kinetic heating. Choice of cruising speed and structural temperature are coupled and determine the material used in manufacturing. (BAe Systems)

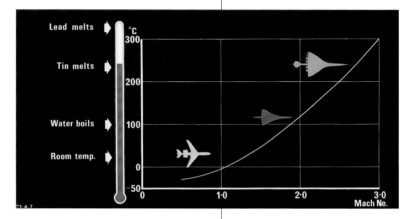

Concorde technology was developed from the military and research aircraft seen here. This will never have to happen again because Concorde and Tu144 data will be available. (BAe Systems)

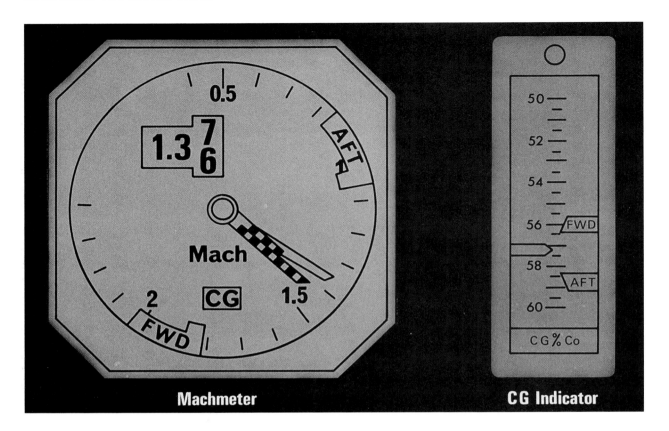

Machmeter **CG Indicator**

The machmeter and CG indicator on Concorde have automatic bugs that show the centre of gravity limits as fuel is pumped aft and forward as flight regime changes. (BAe Systems)

by Dick Fitzsimmons, who headed up the Douglas effort. Indeed Douglas and the other two companies made a number of proposals to the American government and airlines. Through my association with the Society of Experimental Test Pilots and from planned visits in the 1950s to the American west-coast aircraft manufacturers, I made great friends with Bill Magruder, who sadly died in 1974. Bill was a Douglas test pilot on the DC-8 at the time and later moved to Lockheed as their supersonic transport technical manager and project pilot, later becoming Program Director of the American SST to the government in Washington DC. When Bill first went to Lockheed, he seemed to me to become the leading proponent of the SST due to his strong personality and considerable engineering ability. During a visit to Lockheed, Burbank, I had an opportunity to sit in the double delta-wing mock-up, similar to the Concorde configuration, but altogether much bigger. It was a massive monster. Boeing on the other hand favoured the swing wing based on the concept they had used in a competition on a military project (TFX). Designated Model 733, it was altered hundreds of times before emerging as the prototype configuration Model 2707. In its final form it was not very different from its Lockheed competitor.

The first moves towards an SST originated quietly in NACA in 1956 and in December of that year, FAA Administrator General Elwood Quesada received a NACA report stating that there was every reason to go ahead. It is clear that some form of participation by the government was

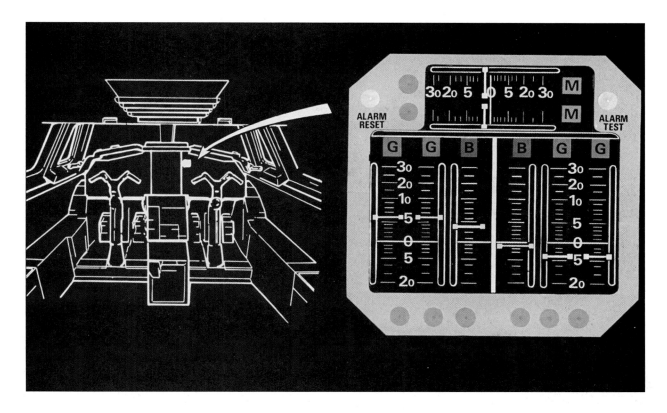

seen as essential for such a venture. Under General Quesada's leadership, the SST programme began to take shape in the summer of 1960. The cancellation of the North American B70 in 1969 was a blow to Quesada but NACA's support had a strong cushioning effect. Subsidising such a programme was of course foreign to a country that relied on free enterprise control, whereas Europe accepted the government's presence. An SST study ordered by the Federal Aviation Administration (FAA) from the United Research Inc. of Cambridge, Massachusetts, predicted that the American aircraft manufacturers should not enter into an SST programme without government support, which would have to compete against Britain, France and Russia.

This was seen as a one-choice situation – 'nationalise' the whole programme. The strong possibility of dominance in the SST field by Britain, France or Russia was too horrifying for America to contemplate. Before his resignation from the FAA, General Quesada had recommended to President Kennedy that $500,000 per week for two years be allocated for the SST research programme and advised that he had awarded study contracts to Pratt and Whitney and General Electric for a SST engine. General Quesada was succeeded by Najeeb Halaby, who later became head of Pan American, a man of strong belief in supersonic transport. Few if any of the major airlines were particularly enthusiastic about being pushed into the supersonic era when they were still paying for their recently acquired subsonic jet transports.

In supersonic flight centre of pressure on wing moves aft, hence the use of trim by movement of fuel. Concorde is trimmed to fly with ½° down elevon in cruise. A control position indicator is provided to show position of elevons and whether the controls are in blue, green hydraulic systems or mechanical signalling. (BAe Systems)

North American B70 supersonic bomber prototype flying from Edwards Air Force Base, California. This project was cancelled in 1969. (P. March)

Al White, Chief Test Pilot of North American, flew the B70 on its first flight and subsequently worked for TWA. (Author)

President Kennedy's declared intent to get a man to the moon and back before 1970 was no secret. But it came as a great surprise when, following a favourable report from the Supersonic Transport Advisory Group and from a Cabinet-level committee under Vice-President Johnson, President Kennedy dropped his bombshell on 5 June 1963 at the Air Force Academy when he confirmed that the SST programme would go ahead. Some members of the Senate never got to grips with the concept of cancelling the B70 but at the same time subsidising the SST, but now the race was on. Another test-pilot friend of mine, Al White, flew the B70 on its first flight and became a member of the Supersonic Transport Advisory Group.

Trans World Airlines (TWA) stole the march on Pan American by ordering a fleet of six of SSTs. Pan American had in the meantime put the cat among the pigeons by ordering six Concordes. Early indications gave a first flight date of the US SST in 1967. TWA expected delivery of the first production model certificated not later that 1 January 1971. Both TWA and Pan American made down payments to confirm their orders.

As time went on, the US SST got bigger with a requirement to fly 4,000 miles with a payload of 40,000lbs. The competing designs were the Lockheed double delta – very sleek and the fastest of the contenders with a cruise of M=3.0; the Boeing swing wing at M=2.7; and North American civil version of the B70. In due course, the choice was narrowed to Lockheed and Boeing and finally on 31 December 1996 Boeing was chosen to build a SST prototype, probably more because of its achievements with the Boeing 707 and their reputation with airlines rather than pure technical merit. Some $511 million had been spent to date and another $142 million was requested. This resulted in furious debate in the Senate, where demands were made that the project be killed outright or at least postponed. Senator William Proxmire, a longtime enemy of the SST, called for a major reduction in funding. It was believed that the Concorde and the Russian Tupolev Tu144 would fly in 1968 and therefore, on the eve of an election year, cancellation of the US SST would be a political catastrophe. At an earlier stage proposals to arrange international collaboration had been aired but responses from the USA were generally negative. A British Government minister, Peter Thorneycroft, actually approached Elwood Quesada with a 'you join us, we join you' proposal. This received a 'don't call us, we'll call you' type of response. A similar approach to Najeeb Halaby by the British Ambassador to the United States, Sir Harold Caccia, was made on the basis that there might not be room for two SSTs, but this received an equally unbending response.

The saga continued for the next few years with growing concern on both sides of the Atlantic about the escalating costs. BAC made it clear to Boeing that Boeing's participation would be welcome but that major changes to the design would be difficult. None of it happened and the Anglo-French Agreement of 1962 overtook events, leaving a clear impression that the USA wished to go it alone. The Anglo-French Agreement itself had been preceded by an open-ended report to the Cabinet that did not recommend a decision either way. Julian Amery (Minister of Aviation) argued strongly for the project. Looking at all the to-ing and fro-ing that took place, I do not believe anyone including Prime Minister Harold Macmillan knew what to do but the agreement really ended any thought of American collaboration. The matter did not immediately die. Halaby in particular was not slow to

Russian Tu144, made by Tupolev, landing at Paris. The prototype did not incorporate the canard (fore-plane) clearly visible in this photograph. (Jonathan Falconer)

remind the President of the dangers of leaving the British and French to proceed unchallenged. In his own words, he talked of 'relinquishing world civil transport leadership'.

Tied into this conundrum was the return of the Harold Wilson government (newly elected, but narrowly) which, faced with many economic problems, desired to extract itself from 'prestige projects' and made it clear that it wished to re-examine the Concorde scheme. Following a visit to the UK, Halaby predicted that 'the next financial climax will occur after the British election when the United Kingdom will have an agonising re-appraisal of the rising costs of the development of Concorde'. (The 'e' at the end of Concorde was added in December 1967.) As will be noted later, the lack of any break clause in the Anglo-French Agreement led to a reluctant continuation by the British. Recently Lord Jenkins, who was Minister of Aviation at the time, indicated his feeling that ideas of collaboration with the USA were only semi-serious. In fact, at the first meeting between Harold Wilson and President Johnson, the SST was not even mentioned. Thanks to the British reluctance in some quarters, the French would have liked to go it alone, providing some level of American collaboration and a non-British engine could be found.

The USA made strenuous efforts to keep abreast of Concorde's programme and associated problems. Timing between the entry into service of Concorde and the US SST was regarded as being particularly important. A two-year gap was considered to be acceptable but three was not. Even the CIA were involved in gathering intelligence, which was passed via the FAA to the President's Advisory Committee on a regular basis and irregularly by other interested parties.

At a recent witness seminar on Concorde run by the Institute of Contemporary British History Lord Jenkins of Hillhead stated that he was not conscious of any pressure from the USA to cancel Concorde. That, of course, is not to say that some gentle persuasion behind the scenes was not exerted on Julian Amery and on Denis Healey when he was Minister of Defence during the period 1964–70.

In 1968 the American presidential election was won by the Republican candidate Richard Nixon. During the briefings to the new administration, the FAA admitted that the US SST had evolved from the challenge posed by Concorde. At this time there were 78 options for Concorde and 122 for the American SST, of which 58 were attributed to foreign airlines. Since 1967, the Federal Aviation Agency (formerly called the Federal Aviation Administration) had become part of a new Department of Transport. President Nixon continued with the US SST with some difficulty in September 1969, by which time Concorde and the Tu144 had flown. Further studies by the FAA assumed a certification of Concorde in late 1972 and the President had announced an entry into service date for the US SST of 1978, thus providing the opportunity for sales of 200 or more Concordes or Tu144s. It was thought that 240 Concordes could be produced and delivered with the US SST production starting in 1978 and reaching 500 by 1990. The Tu144 sales would come from the Concorde market, although the majority of them would be required by the Soviet carrier Aeroflot.

By 1970 the US SST was in big trouble, although Bill Magruder, newly appointed as Program Director, fought with gusto to save the project. He

Bill Magruder, ex-Douglas and Lockheed test pilot, was supersonic adviser to the American government. He went on to become President of Piedmont Airlines. (BAe Systems)

Concorde in British Airways' new colours taking off from Filton on the thirtieth anniversary of Concorde 002's first flight. (BAe Systems)

spent time with Sir George Edwards and he flew twice in Concorde 002 with me. This enabled him to substantiate his arguments, which he made to a large number of organisations in the USA. Senator Proxmire loomed large and dangerous on the scene, especially when the Senate rejected further funding for SST. However, this was compromised and extended to March 1971. I stayed at Bill Magruder's house in Washington DC on the fateful weekend of cancellation. In spite of all his efforts, funding was deleted on 18 March. An amendment to restore was also defeated. The US SST was dead. What few people realise is that the USA spent more money – and finished up with nothing – than was ever spent on Concorde. Bill Magruder went on to become President of Piedmont Airlines.

But that was not the end of the story. 'Ban the Concorde' became a reality on the back of noise regulations and the ban on supersonic flight over the USA. Both were hotly contended by the British and French governments, according to Kenneth Owen's book *Concorde and the Americans*. It may appear surprising that over-land supersonic operation was part of Anglo-French thinking but the routes that I am aware of were from the northern extremities, across Canadian open country and on to Los Angeles and San Francisco. (The matter of landing permission in the USA is covered later.)

As already stated, experience of supersonic flight was based on data gained from research and military aircraft. Such an experience will never need to happen again because the technology of Concorde and the Russian Tu144 is available, although some of the lessons will show how not to create a future AST because technology has developed very rapidly in the intervening period. Even so, this should not be taken as an open invitation to design engineers to start with a totally fresh piece of paper. The achievement of the basic goal of Concorde required great innovation, patience and dedicated determination. Many obstacles had to be overcome. Politics played a major role and working with another nation was a task in itself.

ORGANISATION AND RESPONSIBILITIES

The complexity of Concorde was only matched by that of the organisation behind it. There were times when to coin an old expression of my days at Vickers-Armstrong, 'it seemed a bloody funny way to run a railroad!'. However, as the project was totally Government funded and was entirely new in concept, this was not particularly surprising. It is almost easier to list those who were not involved than those who were. The basis of the organisation was six partners (two governments, two airframe companies and two engines companies), supposedly working on a 50/50 split on costs, work and management. In simple language, no single person was in charge and needless to say management by committee was the result.

There were two committees on the constructors' side: the Airframe Committee and the Engine Committee, with senior posts alternating every two years.

AIRFRAME COMPANY		ENGINE COMPANY
General André Puget	*Chairman/MD*	Sir Arnold Hall
Sir George Edwards	*Vice-Chairman/Deputy MD*	H.A. Desbruères
Pierre Satrè	*Technical Director*	E.J. Warlow-Davies
Sir Archibald Russell	*Deputy Technical Director*	M. Garnier
J.F. Harper	*Director of Production/Controls*	R. Able
Louis Giusta	*Deputy Director Production/Controls*	W.F. Saxton
A.H.C. Greenwood	*Sales Director*	—
W.J. Jakimiuk	*Sales Director*	—
G.E. Knight	*Director*	J. Bloch
B.C. Vallières	*Director*	H.W. Rees

The next layer included Dr Bill Strang and Lucien Servanty, Chief Engineers. Under them a special team consisting of Mick Wilde, Doug Thorne and Doug Vickery from BAC and Gilbert Cormery, Etienne Farge and Jean Resch from Sud was formed. They represent the very highest calibre of design engineers and Concorde's qualities are the result of their talents. One other person who did a tremendous job in generating enthusiasm, total

The author signing a Concorde photograph for the Minister of Technology Tony Benn with Sir James Hamilton, Director General Concorde, looking on. (BAe Systems)

André Turcat with the author on the occasion of 001's roll out in December 1967. (BAe Systems)

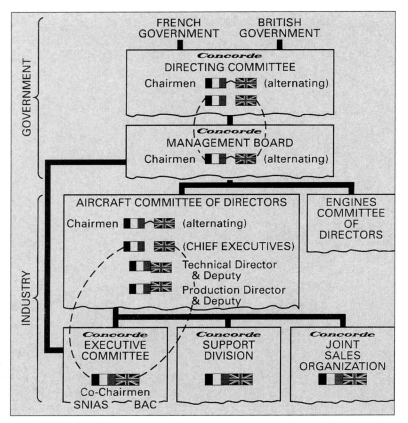

FRENCH GOVERNMENT   BRITISH GOVERNMENT

Concorde
DIRECTING COMMITTEE
Chairmen ▮▮▶≫≪ (alternating)

Concorde
MANAGEMENT BOARD
Chairmen ▮▮▶≫≪ (alternating)

AIRCRAFT COMMITTEE OF DIRECTORS
Chairmen ▮▮▶≫≪ (alternating)
▮▮ ≫≪ (CHIEF EXECUTIVES)
▮▮ ≫≪ Technical Director & Deputy
▮▮ ≫≪ Production Director & Deputy

ENGINES COMMITTEE OF DIRECTORS

Concorde
EXECUTIVE COMMITTEE
▮▮ ≫≪
Co-Chairmen
SNIAS   BAC

Concorde
SUPPORT DIVISION
▮▮ ≫≪

Concorde
JOINT SALES ORGANIZATION
▮▮ ≫≪

GOVERNMENT

INDUSTRY

British and French government organisation for the Concorde project. (BAe Systems)

Opposite: Prototypes 001 and 002 and preproduction 01 seen at Fairford. The production visor arrangement is clearly visible on 01, flanked by the two prototypes. (BAe Systems)

confidence among those concerned and assisting in the language problems was Paul Cameron, who sadly died in a motor accident.

During the time of Concorde development there were far fewer changes at the top within BAC than in Sud, which went through the process of merging with Nord. There were many outstanding individuals in both teams. An immediate rapport existed between General Puget and Sir George Edwards, which proved to be the saving of Concorde on a number of occasions. This was especially so during the heated arguments between Russ (Sir Archibald Russell) and Pierre Satrè and Lucien Servanty, who wanted to build a medium-range SST called the Super Caravelle, whereas Russ was always convinced that nothing short of transatlantic range was any good. Some arguments escalated into actual rows between Russ and Satrè on this fundamental difference of technical judgement. There was no immediate winner and the two-version concept appeared in the Anglo-French Agreement until common sense prevailed.

Without the understanding and respect that General Puget and Sir George Edwards had for one another Concorde would probably not have survived. There was great sadness and anger on the British side when General Puget, who had been the wartime commander of Free French bomber squadrons based in the UK and who therefore knew and liked the British, was despatched as French Ambassador to Sweden, supposedly as punishment for the rising costs of Concorde. He was succeeded by Maurice Papon, a former Paris Prefect of Police who is better known for his misdemeanours during the Second World War in connection with persecution of the Jews. In 1968 he was succeeded by General Henri Ziegler, an old colleague of BAC's from his days with Air France and on the Jaguar programme. By the time he went, the work on Concorde was virtually complete.

The beginning of the collaboration was not an easy task in itself. Nationalism was present on both sides and each party harboured suspicions that the other was trying to do them down. Some of this distrust rubbed off on personal relationships, but this changed when 001 and 002 began to fly and when 01 and 02 started world-wide visits. When 001 and 002 joined up over the Paris Air Show in 1969, Sir George remarked on that memorable day: 'if anyone starts niggling about the British and French again, I'll remind them of what they've seen today'.

My first impressions of Toulouse were somewhat coloured by the presence of the Duke of Edinburgh, whom I had flown to Toulouse in a

BAC 1-11 on 4 November 1965 for an official visit. I was most impressed by our welcome and enjoyed travelling in a car with my co-pilot Denis Hayley-Bell headed by two out-riders on motorcycles. By contrast, my next trip was a bit different when my party had to find a taxi to take us from the airport side to the factory.

At Filton my early meetings with André Turcat were predominantly concerned with the flight-deck layout. This was a bit of a mismatch because BAC was responsible for the layout but Sud was responsible for most of the equipment and André Turcat was adamant about the need for a moving map display. He was usually accompanied by Jacques Guiguard, Chief Test Pilot, and Michel Retief, Chief Flight Engineer. Jacques Guiguard was a most charming man, who had experienced two very major crashes in the Trident II and had the scars to prove it. Everyone took an immediate liking to him and we at BAC were very sorry when he retired on health grounds soon after the first flight of 001, on which he was co-pilot. Among some of the French officials I suspect there was a feeling that to have someone so battered involved with the programme was not good for Concorde's image. If this is true, then it is sheer nonsense and we certainly did not react in this way. It took me a little time to get acquainted with André Turcat, a most competent and able test pilot-cum-engineer, for whom I had great respect, and we formed a close working relationship and friendship.

Michel Retief soon showed that he was another highly gifted individual with many constructive suggestions for the layout of the various systems panels. The fuel system was a typical example. Russ nearly went mad over the telephone when I agreed that Michel Retief's layout for it was better than that proposed by our head fuel-system designer, Tom Boucher, and Russ accused me of putting the programme back nine months. Such outbursts were part of Russ's make-up. He was undoubtedly the father of Concorde on the British side and took over as Chairman of the Concorde Airframe Committee of Directors from Sir George during 1969. The chairmanship alternated on an annual basis between BAC and Sud.

The language difficulties experienced by many improved with time as a result of attendance at night school to learn French – the French always seemed better at learning English than we were at French. But even so-called experts had to be careful at meetings and on decision-making occasions because the French vocabulary is smaller than ours, which can lead to misinterpretation. Bill Strang worked pretty well with Satrè while Servanty, who most of the time pretended not to speak English and who refused to fly, limiting his attendance at meetings was not so straightforward. Over a gradual period, many friendships grew up at almost every level, although the use of Christian names took time and visits to one another's homes even longer. But it all came together thanks to a great deal of understanding and patience. The SEPECAT Jaguar and the MRCA programmes (of which the latter became the Panavia Tornado) benefited from the Concorde experience.

We were supposed to create an integrated organisation and I remember André Turcat and I were directed to do so by British and French officials. We played around with this idea for a bit, but concluded that with two flight centres 400 miles apart it was impractical. We decided that two parallel organisations were the right solution and that is what we had.

Both prototypes were equipped with extensive flight-test information. Three flight-test observer positions were located in the front fuselage. (BAe Systems)

When the Flight Test meeting (at which our integration directive was supposed to have been complied with) took place at Toulouse with a French official, Monsieur Dumas, in the chair, André Turcat waited until we were packing up to catch the aircraft back to Filton before he informed Monsieur Dumas that we had two parallel organisations, not an integrated one. Dumas threw all his papers in the air and said 'Now you tell me!'. That was the last we heard of it.

The name Concorde was submitted to Sir George via Charles Gardner, Publicity Manager at BAC, from F.G. Clark, the Publicity Manager at Filton, by telephone, but giving credit to his son who was at Cambridge University. The 'e' gave no problem for Sir George and Charles Gardner, would obviously please General Puget, and looked better in any case. But it does not seem that there was any consultation about this with our Government: Julian Amery was furious and the British officials decreed that the aircraft would be called 'Concord'. True to his word to General Puget, Sir George stuck to his guns, so a ridiculous situation arose which lasted until 001 roll-out in December 1967, when all BAC public information on Concorde carried the 'e' and all the details from the British Government did not. At 001's roll-out, Tony Wedgwood Benn gave official blessing to the restoration of the 'e' as a mark of the great milestone in Anglo-French collaboration.

The British Government's direction of the programme was vested in the Concorde Directing Committee through to the Administrative and Technical Sub-Committee. This changed in 1968 with the formation of the Concorde Management Board. Over the critical period of 1966–70, Sir James Hamilton was Director-General of the Concorde Division at the Ministry of Aviation and we were extremely lucky to have a man of such great ability and understanding at the helm. Bernard Lathière, who was Chairman of Airbus for many years, held a similar position in France

In an effort to co-ordinate common requirements for cockpit layout, choice of systems and equipment, and everything else required for airline operation, maintenance and servicing, a committee of airline vice-presidents under the chairmanship of Bill Mentzer of United Airlines was formed to work along similar lines to the system devised for the Boeing 747.

The Mentzer Committee was approved by the Committee of Directors. In retrospect, I am not sure how much it achieved other than increasing the number of meetings, although one was introduced to some splendid people in the process. There were numerous meetings with all the option holders, which were extremely onerous because hitherto there had been very little airline input into the cockpit layout, for instance. The cockpit layout was complicated by the fact that a number of people (not airlines), including André Turcat, wanted a moving map display as already mentioned. This equipment was a relic of that specified for TSR2 and made by Sagem-Ferranti. It dwarfed the whole layout and was totally unnecessary for a civil aircraft, which would spend most of its time flying over the sea. Needless to say, it was thrown out of the prototype layout for the production aircraft and replaced by a set of conventional engine instruments on the pilot's front centre panel. There was further complication in that Gordy Granger, engineering technical pilot for TWA, wanted all instruments to be of the 'strip type' but all his powers of

Bill Strang, BAC Technical Director, who played such an important role in the Concorde programme. (BAe Systems)

The late Michael Crisp, Flight Test Manager at Vickers Armstrong, British Aircraft Corporation and British Aerospace for many years, during which time he was involved in the Viscount, Vanguard, BAC1-11, VC10 and Concorde projects, to name but a few. (BAe Systems)

BAe flight-test team with Concorde 002 at RAF Fairford. The author is standing at the front in orange overalls. (BAe Systems)

persuasion failed to convince his other airline counterparts. These flight-deck meetings were a real nightmare. My heart still bleeds for Doug Vickery, Frank Verrier and Stan Lock on the design side.

When it came to flying, the Concorde prototype was treated as a military aircraft and approval came from the Director of Flying at the Ministry of Technology under rules defined in Air Publication AVP67, modified for Concorde. This also included approval of the test pilots concerned. In September 1970, the British and French authorities (Ministry of Aviation, Air Registration Board, Service Technique Aéronautique and Secrétariat Général a l'Aviation Civile) produced a publication defining the procedures for authorisation of flight during development and for eventual certification. The result was even more committees. First came the Concorde Airworthiness Committee (CAC) made up of the four main contractors and their opposite numbers from the official services. Second was the Joint Certification Committee (JCC) consisting of the members of the CAC, plus one extra member from the Air Registration Board (ARB). Third was the Flight Test Committee (CDV) formed with the Flight Test Group (FTG) underneath it. The FTG started as: M.J. Renaudie – Head of French Delegation; M.A. Cavin – Centre d'essais en vol (CEV); M.P. Dudal – Test Pilot (CEV); M.F. Gillon – Toulouse; H.J. Allwright – Head of British Delegation; J.C. Chaplin – ARB; S.G. Corps – Test Pilot (ARB); H.J. Keyes – Ministry of Aviation and Supply.

The CAC and national head of CDV had the right to delay the execution of any test, if the safety conditions were considered to be unsatisfactory. They also laid down exhaustive procedures for the authorisation of first flights and for engine clearance before Certificates of Airworthiness were issued. The so-called 'Grand Livre' procedure was adopted within the definition 'TSS Standard No. 0-2 requires the constructors to prepare a certification compliance register as evidence of compliance with airworthiness requirements'. 'Grand Livre' was the fancy title for a document consisting of a collection of sheets, each sheet recording compliance of a single system or single zone of the aircraft with one requirement of TSS standards. There were constant changes on the official side but some streamlining did take place on formation of the Concorde Management Board and further modifications were made in 1971.

The FTG remained fairly intact, although Pierre Dudal, an Air France Training Captain who was put through the French Air Force Test Pilot School, gradually faded out with back problems caused by his ejection from the Mirage IV attached to André Turcat's team at Toulouse. He was replaced by Captain Gilbert Defer (CEV) who later joined Aérospatiale and finally became Chief Test Pilot. The use of certification test pilots like Gordon Corps for Government participation was strongly disapproved of by D.P. Davies, who was Chief Test Pilot ARB, but he was overruled for once. FTG carried out several special flights during each phase of development and participated in the route proving. The ARB flew each production aircraft before delivery to British Airways (BA) following a similar pattern to the French practice. There was nothing in the 'rules' that said they had to and I fell out with Gordon Corps when he was unable to fly a BA delivery at the appropriate time due to other commitments. When I told him that I was going to deliver it without his flight, he rapidly changed his diary. I had become quite accustomed to ARB pilots making 'rules' as they went along over many years of experience, but I was not prepared to buy this one. Normally, we all got on extremely well with much mutual respect.

The manufacture of all major components at British and French factories respectively. These components were then transported to the assembly lines at Filton and Toulouse. (BAe Systems)

The Director of Flying at the Ministry of Technology organised the whole network of test routes on the UK side and his French counterpart did likewise. A joint document covering this aspect was issued by the Director of Flying at the Ministry of Technology and the Director of the French Flight Test Centre, making full use of military radar stations in addition to the civil ones, thus enabling all the early flying to be conducted under full radar coverage. All ground installations were equipped so that a common VHF frequency of 142.15 megacycles could be used throughout each flight. However, radar coverage was not available for much of the intake control system test flights when flying south from Casablanca or Tangier.

Within BAC it was necessary to set up an entirely new organisation at Fairford covering flight test, maintenance, inspection, test services, design support and all other supporting services such as security, telephone operators, canteen staff etc. The Filton flight-test department needed boosting anyway as it was too small, although the quality of its work was very high. Moving the majority of the flight test and test pilots from Wisley cured this problem and brought recent civil experience into the department. Fairford personnel, including representatives from Rolls-Royce, SNECMA, Aérospatiale and Government, peaked at nearly 500. The whole flight-test centre was answerable to me as Director of Flight Test, while certain individuals also retained responsibility to their respective departments at Filton. Bob McKinlay came in as Assistant Director, as did stalwarts from Wisley, Mike Crisp, Mike Bailey, Roy Holland and several others. Test Pilots John Cochrane, Peter Baker, Johnnie Walker and Eddie McNamara joined the programme immediately, later to be followed by Roy Radford, who had a large BAC1-11 to programme to complete at the start of Fairford.

The responsibilities in collaborative projects normally promote much argument as to who does what. The 50/50 split of Concorde was as follows:

The author and Roy Radford, who succeeded him as Chief Test Pilot in 1982, seated on the flightdeck of Concorde 002, January 1973. (BAe Systems)

	SUD AVIATION AÉROSPATIALE		BRITISH AIRCRAFT CORPORATION BRITISH AEROSPACE
Design			
			Performance
		Aerodynamics	Aerodynamics
Stability		Lateral	Longitudinal
Systems		Hydraulics	Electrics
		Pneumatics	Fuel
		Air generation	Air distribution
			Anti ice
			Powerplant
Manufacture			
	Centre fuselage		Nose and Forebody
	Centre wing		Rear fuselage and fin
			Nacelles
			Wingtips

Essentially, the largest proportion of the British share was the powerplant, while Sud (Aérospatiale) was responsible for the wing and handling qualities. The tasks allocated to each development aircraft was supposed to reflect this but a more flexible approach had to be adopted in practice.

The manufacturing of the various components grew fairly easily out of this split. Contrary to common belief the only duplication was the two assembly lines at Filton and Toulouse. The individual components were manufactured throughout all the company factories and shipped to the assembly points by road, sea or occasionally by air in the Guppy. The large hangar built for the Bristol Brabazon was used for Concorde assembly at Filton. This great hangar was more of an assembly area than an assembly line due to its physical layout. Consequently, the British aircraft were assembled in-situ, whereas Toulouse built a new assembly shed for Concorde so that a genuine line existed. This later became the start of the Airbus facility at Toulouse.

The flight-test aircraft carried various amounts of test instrumentation for recording flight data. The wiring associated with these installations amounted to several miles on the prototypes, with a small reduction on the preproduction aircraft.

The original drawings for the aircraft were in French and English showing both centimetres and inches. When it came to mating major components, there was a general sigh of relief that there were no yawning gaps. The standard of engineering was extremely high and join-ups went exceptionally well. The manufacture of the powerplant was split between BAe, Rolls-Royce (Filton) and SNECMA at Villaroche near Paris. As explained later, the powerplant was a single integrated unit. Air transport in the form of an Argosy freighter was used extensively for moving completed engines from Rolls-Royce at Filton to and from France.

One particular area of organisation that fell down badly at the beginning was that of communication. It appeared to me that the fundamental need for people involved in every aspect of the project to move easily between the UK and France had been totally underestimated. The number of

President Pompidou meeting British Ambassador Christopher Soames at Toulouse after flying from Paris in 001 with 002 positioned at Toulouse as part of the reception committee, May 1971. (BAe Systems)

Concorde with Airbus Guppy, which was used for transporting airframe components on some occasions. (BAe Systems)

Roll-out of the first preproduction 01 G-AXDN at Filton, November 1971. (BAe Systems)

The electrical wiring on Concorde, especially the flight-test instrumentation wiring, amounted to many miles. (BAe Systems)

Concorde under construction at Filton. (BAe Systems)

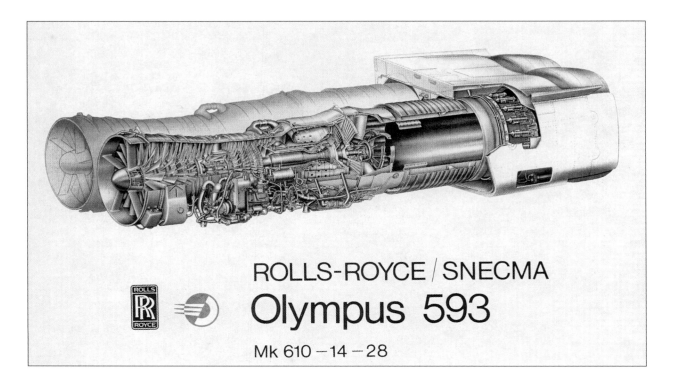

ROLLS-ROYCE / SNECMA
Olympus 593
Mk 610 — 14 — 28

Concorde is powered by four Olympus 593 Mk610 engines located in pairs under each wing and producing 38,050lbs thrust each. (Rolls-Royce)

communication aircraft available was small, and they were antiquated. Sud used a Nord 262 and a small Paris four-seater, while BAC (Filton) provided a Hunting President (the civil version of the Pembroke). The journey time took several hours and a great deal of the travel was done by airlines. However, there were no direct flights to Toulouse, so all journeys were via Paris from Heathrow or Bristol (Lulsgate). The result was that it took the best part of two days to cover a meeting that probably only needed 2 hours. The cost in time, travel and hotel expenses was consequently very high. By 1968 common sense had prevailed with the purchase of an HS125 eight-seat executive aircraft, used to make two round trips per day between Filton and Toulouse. Rolls-Royce also acquired an HS125 which BAC used to borrow on occasions. Communication between Weybridge and Filton was vastly improved by the use of a fourteen-seat Heron, in place of a car journey that might take 5 hours. Unfortunately, communication aircraft and their use have always been a prime target for accountants. Over my many years in the aircraft industry, I have got used to the reduction in communication aircraft always being on the agenda after 'tea and biscuits' in any cost-cutting exercise.

One other area that required special attention was that of translation. There was no shortage of paperwork on Concorde and translating French documentation into English and vice-versa became a major task. A team of translators was employed for this and they also acted as interpreters at meetings. Simultaneous translation systems were only just beginning to appear.

SPECIAL ASPECTS

T he peculiar demands of a supersonic transport resulted in many special considerations, so in order to give an accurate portrayal of the Concorde story some of these will be highlighted here. Equally, it is neither necessary nor the intention of this book to describe in detail the whole anatomy of Concorde.

STRUCTURES AND CHOICE OF MATERIALS

History will show that the choice of M=2.0/2.2 as cruise speed was a very wise decision on the part of the STAC and the manufacturers. The structure of an aircraft flying at supersonic speeds becomes hot due to the kinetic heating caused by skin friction. It is therefore fundamental to choose a cruising speed that is compatible with the temperature properties of the metals to be used in the aircraft's construction. At subsonic speeds the structural temperature in cruise is normally about -35°C but at M=2.0/2.2 the kinetic heating effect raises it to approximately 120°C, while at M=3.0 it just about doubles to 250°C. The latter could not be tolerated by aluminium alloys and would necessitate the use of steel and/or titanium, but fabrication using these materials posed major technical problems and high cost. Consequently, there is only limited use of steel and titanium in one or two special parts of Concorde, for example in the powerplant. Later, knowledge gained from the Bristol 188 and North American B70 experiences gave little encouragement to adopt the higher speed and higher temperature conditions and substantiated the STAC's original view, which was supported by the manufacturers. The STAC firmly believed that the use of aluminium alloys would enable this country to be among the leaders in the supersonic transport field.

The long-range version of Concorde started out as a M=2.2 transport. This required an in-flight demonstration of M=2.35 associated with a temperature of 425° Kelvin. However, it was soon calculated that reduction to M=2.05 and 400° Kelvin would give a substantial improvement in fatigue life, while only lengthening journey time by a small amount. I always draw a sigh of relief when I think back to this decision. I believe that Concorde would not have achieved clearance of M=2.35 without substantial changes to the intakes in particular. As it was, a maximum speed just above M=2.2 was achieved during the flight-test programme only by means of manual intervention by the crew of N1/N2 relationship of the engine, in order to avoid engine surge. The N1 was wound down manually to such a reduced value that there was no more puff available to go any faster. Normally, the relationship between N1 and N2 is automatically scheduled to achieve

First preproduction aircraft 01 G-AXDN under final assembly at Filton. (BAe Systems)

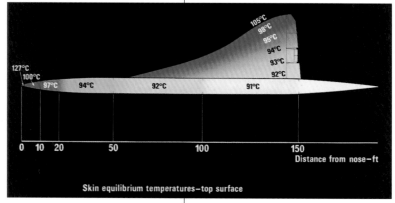

Skin temperatures experienced by Concorde in supersonic flight. (BAe Systems)

greatest efficiency in fuel consumption. Manual intervention widened the gap and increased surge margin (see p. 90).

In order to establish a safe fatigue life taking account of the heating and subsequent cooling of the structure in a typical flight cycle, a special facility was constructed at RAE Farnborough into which a complete Concorde fuselage with wing was installed. This became known as the Concorde Fatigue Specimen. It was heated and cooled by means of thermal piping to represent a flight cycle of take-off, climb, cruise at M=2.0, descent and landing. The plan was that these tests would precede the oldest aircraft in the programme by a substantial margin. When the tests were terminated, Concorde was cleared for just over 20,000 cycles as this was considered to be sufficient, although it was appreciated that a further extension would be possible by methods of inspection and data obtained from aircraft in service. Normally the fatigue life of an aircraft is determined by dividing test results by two, but in the case of Concorde, because of its advanced nature, the figure was three. Hence an initial fatigue life of 6,700 cycles was calculated. As other methods were known to be available, the very high costs of the RAE facility became unattractive.

Indeed, further work covering all the aspects mentioned including re-examination of the RAE results extended Concorde's life to 8,500 cycles. At current utilisation, this will permit operation of the oldest aircraft to about the year 2007. This date can of course be varied by reducing services, however BA has now approved funds to cover the cost of identifying the work necessary to extend to 10,000 cycles, which equates to about the year 2013. Additional work can then extend Concorde's life expectancy further but no doubt will very much depend on whether or not the aircraft is still making a profit.

A second complete aircraft was installed at CEAT Toulouse for static strength test. Numerous other structural test specimens were used in the overall structural programme. The move from 6,700 cycles to 8,500 cycles required twenty-four areas to be investigated in order to confirm predictions. Eighteen of these were perfect, while six need one or slightly more than one inspection. The same routine will be required for the next step to 10,000 cycles, for which a commercial case will be tabled. This process can continue, although each step will need more work than its predecessor.

Materials used in the construction of Concorde. (BAe Systems)

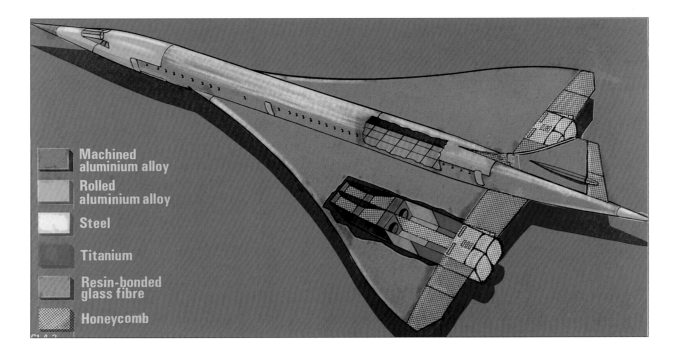

Machined aluminium alloy

Rolled aluminium alloy

Steel

Titanium

Resin-bonded glass fibre

Honeycomb

AERODYNAMICS

In supersonic cruise the exchange rates between drag and weight are very severe. For every additional 1lb of weight, 2lb of fuel is required. When the payload is only a small percentage of all-up weight (5.5 per cent for Concorde) the effect on payload of any increase in drag is extremely penalising. Consequently, close attention had to be paid to profile, interference and excrescence drag.

The evolution of the Concorde's slender ogical delta (ogee) wing plan form was the result of extensive research and development by the STAC. Some 300 test models were used in this process. There were concerns that any break-up of a wind-tunnel model might damage the M=2.0 tunnel at the National Physical Laboratory, so as a result test models using this facility had to be solid. The era in which this work was carried out involved the use of 'knife and fork methods', whereas today it would all be done by computer.

The Ministry of Supply also authorised two research aircraft. For low-speed research specification X197, Handley Page produced the HP115 (flown in 1961). The second aircraft, specification ER193D, was a conversion of the Fairey Delta 2, designated as the BAC 211, in which Peter Twiss had captured the world speed record and was to be used for both low- and high-speed investigation of the 'ogee' wing. It was flown at Filton by Godfrey Auty on 1 May 1965. Both the HP115 and the BAC221 were located at Aero

Flight, RAE Bedford, following initial flights at the manufacturers' airfields in order to contribute to the research study of a slender delta 'ogee' wing. The HP115 was really a glider with a small engine.

Overall aircraft efficiency was fundamental in order to achieve operating costs that were commercially realistic and viable. Overall aircraft efficiency is a function of the lift/drag ratio combined with the efficiency of the powerplant. Whereas lift/drag falls rapidly at speeds between M=0.8 and M=1.0, it only decreases slowly to M=2.0 and to M=3.0. On the other hand, the propulsive efficiency of the powerplant increases steadily up to M=2.0 and M=3.0. When combined, the loss of overall efficiency in the transonic region is recovered at M=2.0.

As an aircraft passes through the speed of sound (M=1.0) the centre of pressure of the wing moves aft causing a nose-down longitudinal trim change, which would normally be countered by retrimming the flight controls. However, this would cause excessive drag in cruise, so a system of moving the centre of gravity by transferring fuel forward or aft, depending on flight condition, was devised. Thus, Concorde operates within a centre of gravity (CG) envelope that is dependent upon speed.

Changes were made to the shape of the leading edge and the wing tip on the Concorde prototype in order to improve engine surge by reducing the formation of underwing vortices under negative gravity ('g'). The leading edge of the wing apex is subsonic in supersonic cruise. On the prototype wing, the camber was optimised from theory to recuperate the local suction

Handley Page HP115 research aircraft built to examine the low-speed handling aspects of the slender delta configuration. (BAe Systems)

BAC221 taking off from Filton. (BAe Systems)

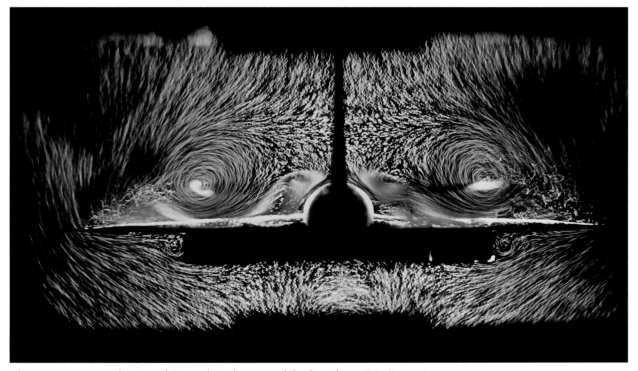

The vortex pattern on the wing of Concorde in the approach/landing phase. (BAe Systems)

Concorde in the advanced state of build, c. 1973. (BAe Systems)

Concorde at the point of rotation on take-off. (BAe Systems)

forces at the angle of attack (at which the leading edge meets the airflow, in this case = 4° in cruise). Only a small reduction in angle of attack moved the stagnation point to the upper surface, which caused a vortex downstream below the wing, thus thickening the boundary layer ahead of intakes and causing surge. It took a year to find this solution, then design and manufacture the revised leading edge for the prototype. Fortunately, the solution was adaptable to the existing leading edge spar. This is a good illustration of the advantages of having a prototype on which such a fundamental change could be tried out in flight as opposed to pure theory.

THE POWERPLANT

The first indoctrination to the method of propelling Concorde through the sky illustrates to the uninitiated that the driving force is an integrated powerplant, not merely an engine, consisting of three main elements: the air intake, the engine and the exhaust system including a reheat (after-burner) system. Development of the Olympus 593 engine that was chosen for Concorde dates back to 1964 when the first 593D derivative engine was developed for bench testing. The history of the Olympus started with Olympus engines for the Avro Vulcan Mk 1 and 2 and the TSR2 supersonic aircraft. The early work on 593D engines demonstrated the basic design concepts, although there were many conflicting studies made covering pressure ratio, fuel consumption, weight, diameter and turbine entry temperature before the 593 was selected for Concorde. In fact the choice of engine for a supersonic civil transport is inevitably a compromise due to the wide range of conditions. Fuel consumption and weight are critical, as the penalty on range is very unforgiving. In an ideal world an engine that starts as a turbofan and then shrinks to a straight turbojet would improve the situation, but was impractical in the days of Concorde development.

The Olympus is a turbojet with two spools (two compressors each driven by its own turbine LP and HP). For its time it was a very good engine, in the opinion of the late Pierre Young, who as engineering director of Olympus 593 contributed so much to the success of the engines. As one of the band of brilliant engineers, he turned into reality what the father of the Olympus, Sir Stanley Hooker, had started. Dr Peter Calder also played a huge part as Chief Development Engineer, along with many others on a list too long to record here.

Three major problem areas come into my mind when I think back to the beginning. The first of these was the 'propensity to break shafts'. This phenomenon was due to a temperature difference between top and bottom during cooling after engine shutdown. On restart, the out of balance shaft could break. Consequently, a procedure known as 'de-bowing' was introduced and is still used by Air France and British Airways in restart situations without sufficient engine cool-down (between 30 minutes and 5 hours). The second was exhaust smoke, which was quite horrendous on the prototypes. This required a change from a cannular combustion chamber to an annular, vaporising type. This cured the smoke but the vaporisers used to fall off with regular monotony. There was such an occurrence when the Prime Minister of Australia, Gough Whitlam, flew from Melbourne to Singapore during route proving. He was very understanding when told that an engine change would be required, which was more than can be said of the British Government minister, Gerald Kaufman, who was also a passenger. The third concerns the matter of noise, which was significantly improved with a new nozzle, Thrust-Reverser Aft (TRA) and other noise-related modifications and procedures.

Titanium and steel are used in the engine. The control system is analogue and the control of it by the pilot is very straightforward, although, due to automation, detailed examination indicates a very complicated arrangement. The pilot's throttle controls the amount of fuel going into the engine electronically and hence the speed (N2) of the high-pressure compressor and turbine. Inputs from engine limiters and E schedules (engine control schedules) are also made. The low-speed compressor and turbine speed (N1) is derived from pressure in the jet pipe acting on the low-speed turbine. This pressure is modulated and is automatically controlled by variation of the primary nozzle to match the engine operating limits at the selected value of N2. The 'swallowing capacity' of the engine is dictated by the N1 and matches the intake geometry. This is referred to as engine/intake matching.

The pilot has the ability to select the mode in which the engine operates by a single switch per engine – take-off, climb and cruise. Where there is no restriction on climb after take-off, i.e. no noise abatement and ATC constraints, the actual throttle levers are left in the fully forward position and

Each pair of engine nacelles is positioned under the wing, incorporating air intake, engine and exhaust nozzles. (BAe Systems)

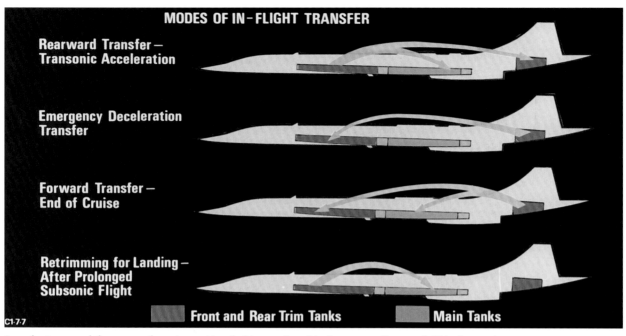

MODES OF IN-FLIGHT TRANSFER

**Rearward Transfer —
Transonic Acceleration**

**Emergency Deceleration
Transfer**

**Forward Transfer —
End of Cruise**

**Retrimming for Landing —
After Prolonged
Subsonic Flight**

C1·7·7

Front and Rear Trim Tanks   Main Tanks

In order to control the centre of gravity position fuel is transferred in the manner illustrated. (BAe Systems)

Vulcan Mk2 used for delta-wing familiarisation of Concorde test pilots. (BAe Systems)

TSR2 powered by Bristol Olympus engines carrying out ground running tests at Boscombe Down, 1964. (BAe Systems)

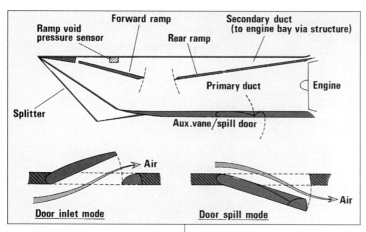

Schematic illustration of the air intake. The inlet mode and spill mode junction of the spill door are also shown. (BAe Systems)

The primary and secondary nozzle arrangement, including the aft thrust reverser (TRA). (BAe Systems)

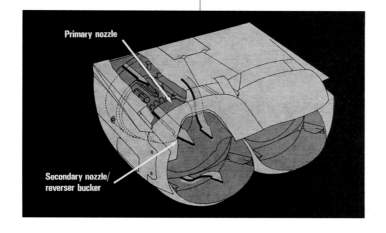

the mode is changed by the mode selection switch. In other words in this ideal situation, which is very rare, the throttles themselves are not retarded until deceleration. In rather crude language this is called 'operating balls to the wall'.

The flight development and certification of the Concorde powerplant was probably the most difficult area in the flight-test programme. The late Dr Bill Strang, BAC Technical Director, once stated that: 'The powerplant was the most persistent area of difficulty, requiring the highest level of sustained and dedicated effort by very talented people to solve the various problems'. He was right and much credit must go to the design group, which contained some real wizards, but once more too many to mention by name.

The long-range cruise requirement called for a finely tuned system with engine handling at least as good as that on subsonic aircraft. The simple two-dimensional rectangular energy units are coupled to the engines of each paired nacelle. Each intake has two ramps (front and rear), a spill door into which an auxiliary inlet is incorporated for use during take-off and up to about M=0.6, and a secondary (bleed) door controlling the secondary flow. The ramps adjust the supersonic inlet compression and subsonic diffuser expansion from M=1.3 upwards. The air going into the engine is provided at approximately M=0.5 at all conditions by this system. Although all the intakes look the same, they are in fact toed-in along the incident lines of entry flows. At supersonic speeds this produces the optimum entry conditions but at take-off with all engines rotating in the same direction, the effect on the blade vibrator modes is markedly different between engines. So much so that N1 on engine four is automatically held down up to 60k, when it is released.

Above M=1.3 the ramps and spill doors are positioned between scheduled maximum and minimum angles determined by intake pressure ratio, Mach numbers, engine speed N1, angle of attack and actual ramp/spill door positions. Changes in ramp angle alter the intake of air and create a shockwave system that originates at the ramp angle and which converges on the lower lip of the intake when optimum configuration of the ramp is reached. Consequently, this is an external compression system and it is this shockwave system that slows down the air entering the intake to M=0.5 as mentioned above. Once the scheduled ramp angle is reached any excess air is dumped through the spill door.

The intake is best described as a self-starting intake, which means that the engine does not lock into surge necessitating engine shut down. Such a system is suitable for speeds of up to about M=2.2 but above this, at M=3.0 for example, a different arrangement would be required. The SR71 Blackbird experience showed the violent nature of an intake 'unstart', which caused the pilot's head to bang against the sides of the cockpit. Intake 'unstarts' are not part of civil aircraft acceptability and designers of future ASTs will do well to remember this.

The Air Intake Control System must satisfy the basic requirements to supply the correct amount of air at high efficiency in a form acceptable to the engine at all flight and engine operating conditions. The primary control parameter is the ratio between Ramp Void Static Pressure and Free Stream Total Pressure, but just think of it as a pressure ratio. Experience on the prototypes brought about a bold change from analogue to digital control late in the development programme, a decision that was vehemently opposed by the French, initially. Modifications to the intakes were extensive before a satisfactory solution to all the problems was achieved. (In-flight engine surge tests are covered in the chapter entitled Flight Development and Certification).

The third main component of the powerplant is the variable nozzle. The two prototypes and first preproduction aircraft were equipped with a conventional-type nozzle as used on a number of military aircraft. A great deal of research work in the area of the nozzle was carried out during

Concorde 202 G-BBDG, the second production model used extensively in the flight-development and certification programme. The TRA nozzle, rear fuselage extension and tail bumper are well illustrated. (BAe Systems)

studies aimed at reducing noise. A major change to the nozzle was made on the second preproduction aircraft onwards with the introduction of the TRA nozzle. This was introduced to save weight and achieve a reduction of noise when the thrust reverser buckets were partially closed.

An innovative feature for a civil aircraft was the introduction of a reheat (after-burner) system in order to augment thrust for take-off and during the transonic acceleration up to M=1.7. This is achieved by squirting fuel into the jet pipe and igniting it. With Concorde the degree of that augmentation is more modest that in the case of military aircraft – 20 per cent increase as compared to about 50 per cent in military aircraft. (Concorde started at 9 per cent and was increased to 20 per cent in stages.)

The use of reheat and variable nozzles produced a new problem in that it was not possible to check correct functioning of the reheat system. On the prototypes this was done by opening up to full power against the brakes and then switching on the reheat. This was not possible on production aircraft because the higher thrust engines caused the wheels to slip, particularly on a wet runway surface, and the blast and noise associated with the prototype procedure were unacceptable for airline service. A revised technique of pre-selecting reheat just prior to brake release was adopted. TSS Standards require a single instrument to show a

A complete fuel-system test rig capable of simulating all combinations of altitude in pitch and roll was installed at Filton so that all cycles of flight could be checked. (BAe Systems)

reading that correlates with engine thrust during take-off and initial climb. Consequently, various engine parameters, intake efficiency, nozzle efficiency and reheat status needed to be brought together. Indication of thrust reverser movement and position was also required.

In order to satisfy these requirements a row of three lights was placed above the primary engine parameters on the pilot's centre panel: Green – clear to go; Amber – 'Con' (Configuration); Blue – 'Rev' (Reverse). As the 'Go' function is not required after take-off, a push button (push to arm and pull to inhibit) is placed next to the lights. At lift-off, the 'go' lights are automatically disarmed, although the button that also arms automatic contingency rating remains in the latched position until reheat is cancelled after take-off.

AIRCRAFT SYSTEMS

The operating environment of Concorde demanded a number of special features and considerations. As before, it is not the purpose of this book to describe every system in detail but some of the background and the most unconventional aspects are summarised below.

On top of its normal function the fuel system served two additional purposes. First, it is used for trimming the aircraft in flight, and second it is

This rare photograph shows how an improperly controlled fuel-transfer test in the hangar at Filton resulted in this 'tail-sitter' – a case of human error – c. 1977. Fortunately, no major damage was done. (BAe Systems)

used as a heat sink for the air-conditioning system. Its complexity was such that a massive rig was installed at Filton so that satisfactory operation of the system could be checked at all possible cycles of flight. The fuel transfer arrangements to control centre of gravity have been mentioned already.

The hydraulic system operates flying control surface actuators, artificial feel units, landing gear, wheel brakes, nosewheel steering, droop nose and visor, engine intake ramps and fuel pumps in the rear transfer tank at 400psi using Oronite M2V fluid. The two main systems and the standby were similar to the de Havilland Comet and Sud Caravelle, and in terms of technology suffer accordingly. I have always regarded the hydraulics as the least satisfactory in an overall assessment of the aircraft's systems. Mysterious fluid transfers have occurred and still do so on occasions. The integrity of hydraulic seals have needed to be strenuously addressed, while the choice of suppliers of the hydraulic pumps provoked vigorous assignations between the British and French involving much in-fighting. Until common sense prevailed, the selection of equipment was one of the least salutory aspects of the Concorde project that emanated from the unbending pursuit of the sacred 50/50 split.

Choice of the electrical generation units came a close second to the hydraulic-pump saga. During the early development of the electrical system, the power required had to be adjusted upwards and 4X60KVA engine-driven brushless alternators are used. Various assessments of up-dating Concorde electronics with modern technology have been made as the weight saving would be substantial. Unfortunately, the cost over such a small fleet of aircraft cannot be justified.

The operating altitude of Concorde requires a cabin differential pressure of 10.7psi, which limits cabin altitude to 11,000ft maximum by means of a cabin-altitude limiter. A cabin pressure limit is set to 11.2psi. The system consists of four independent groups that take air from each high-pressure compressor. The windows on the prototype were the same as the Boeing 707 but had to be reduced in size to meet airworthiness requirements to safeguard against 'window blow-out' at 60,000ft.

The automatic flight-control system (AFCS) is designed to provide 'hands off' capability during climb, cruise and descent down to Category III landing and go-around. The AFCS comprises auto-pilot, auto-throttle, warning and landing displays and an interlock failure monitor. The auto-pilot on the prototype left a lot to be desired and was incapable of coping with sudden atmospheric temperatures changes which resulted in gross overspeeds. When the production version appeared this aspect was still not thought to be satisfactory and BA did not consider that the manufacturers were pursuing a solution with sufficient energy. Consequently, BA formally objected to the granting of a Certificate of Airworthiness at the final meeting of the Airworthiness Review Board (ARB). Their objection was not upheld but the action produced a rapid flight-test programme operating out of Kuala Lumpur and a solution based on use of the auto-throttle system during cruise resulted.

Following Airbus A320 practice, all later Airbus products as well as the Boeing 777 use fly-by-wire, which has become a normal feature of aircraft design. In fact Concorde was fly-by-wire in the sense that movement of the pilot's control column sends an electrical signal to the hydraulic actuators that move the flying control surfaces. At the time of Concorde the

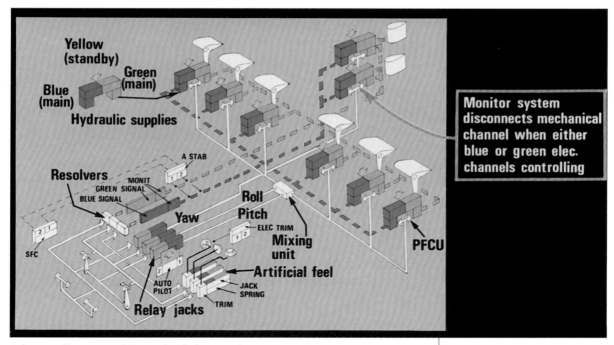

Schematic illustration of Concorde's flight control system. (BAe Systems)

designers were wise to retain a mechanical back-up, and consequently Concorde has a duplicated electrical system with a mechanical mode as back-up in the event of double failure.

Original simulator results showed the aircraft to be uncontrollable following engine failure at M=1.7, producing excessive roll and sideslip sufficient to remove the fin. On this basis the gearing of the elevons was

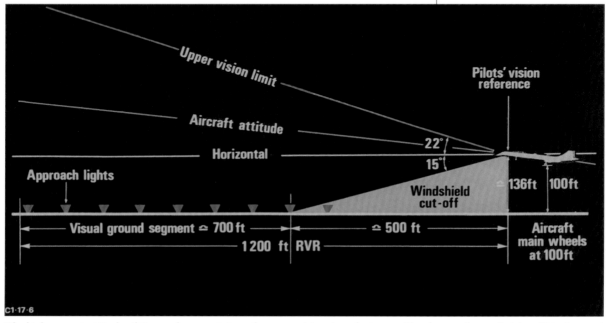

The high nose-up attitude of Concorde necessitates a droop nose/visor in order to provide adequate forward vision. (BAe Systems)

changed on 002 from a ratio 1:1 to 0.3:1. This change necessitated a major redesign of the mixing box unit and was applied to 002, as it was felt that flight to M=2.0 was not safe without the modification. In practice, it was found that the aircraft was not nearly as bad as the simulator showed and in fact 001 was never modified. Indeed 001 was flown to M=2.0 a few days earlier than 002. The gearing on production aircraft was set at 0.7:1. At speeds in excess of max operating (vmo) + 25k the outer elevons are neutralised automatically in order to avoid lateral control reversal. Because the controls are hydraulically operated, artificial feel is created and an auto-stabilisation system is provided in all axes in order to improve the natural stability of the aircraft. The auto-stabilisation system also provides roll/yaw co-ordination in order to reduce side slip angles at slow speed in response to large lateral control demands.

A conventional trim system is provided in all axes. In addition automatic stability correction in the form of Mach Trim, Angle of Attack Trim and Speed Trim is utilised to show compliance with airworthiness requirements. The prototypes were in my view more pleasant to fly because they did not have any of these 'gimmicks'.

Delta wing aircraft do not stall in the conventional sense but wind-tunnel and free-flight models showed that Concorde needed an angle of attack protection system which was developed on 001, consisting of an Angle of Attack Trim, Stick Shaker and Anti-Stall system. The excursions of the free-flight models started at a 30° angle of attack which rapidly increased to 70° where the model became inverted and then thundered back to 30° when the whole process started all over again. Concorde is also equipped with an emergency flight-control system to provide flight control in pitch and roll in the event of a control jam.

An inherent design fault in the power flight-control unit (PFCU) was only revealed on a flight in 002 with Tony Benn, the Minister of Aviation, on board, when I selected one hydraulic to 'off' whereupon an uncontrollable roll began to develop. Switching back to both hydraulic systems rectified the situation but the fault lay in the design of a valve in the PFCU, which took several months to fix while the prototypes remained grounded.

A moveable nose and visor are unique features of Concorde in order to provide adequate vision for take-off and landing, while creating a streamlined aerodynamic shape for climb, cruise and descent. The settings are 5° nose droop for take-off and 12½° (originally 17½°) droop for landing, visor down. After take-off the nose and visor are raised for the whole flight until commencement of initial approach. The arrangement on the prototype was somewhat different in that the visor was metal with a mirror image 'peephole' which gave very limited forward vision, although for reasons that I have never grasped, it met the airworthiness requirements applicable to supersonic transports. I objected to the metal visor when I joined the project but I was led aside and reminded that this was a supersonic transport. Bullshit baffles brains, so goes the saying. In this case the FAA of America made it known to me that they would never certify the aircraft in this configuration. This information concentrated a few minds and Triplex in the UK and in France produced a transparent

Concorde on take-off.
(BAe Systems)

Concorde with undercarriage down and nose drooped prior to landing.
(BAe Systems)

visor in competition. The UK version was adopted following a series of excursions to the top of the Flight Operations building at Filton at night, the height of which equated to Concorde pilots' eye-to-ground height when landing. This change from the prototype was very major in terms of design hours, cost and time. The other problem associated with the prototype was that due to the limited forward vision with the visor up, all subsonic operation was flown visor down. The cockpit noise and vibration at M=0.93 cruise speed was phenomenal. Subsonic cruise speed on production is M=0.95 auto-pilot engaged. Nose droop for landing started at 17½° but was not liked as there was no reference in front of the pilot's eyes and gave the feeling of looking over a precipice. Eventually, 12½° was adopted, which was a good thing because an improvement in directional stability resulted as well.

ENVIRONMENTAL PROBLEMS AND FLIGHT DECK

Sonic Boom

All aircraft flying at supersonic speeds create what is known as a sonic boom, a phenomenon that is often coupled with the 'sound barrier'. As an aircraft flies through the air it creates disturbances in pressure (shock waves) rather akin to the bow-wave of a ship. These shock waves expand at the speed of sound, giving no problem at subsonic speeds, but at M=1.0 and above those pressure waves build up in front of the aircraft to produce an invisible cone about 25 miles wide. The intensity of the boom is dependent on aircraft altitude, weight, wing loading and wing area. This is known as an over-pressure. In the case of Concorde it is about 2lb per sq ft and is spread over a carpet on the ground. In fact, Concorde produces a double boom.

Sonic boom was understood before Concorde appeared on the scene and it was always assumed that supersonic flight over populated areas would be banned, restricting the aircraft to supersonic flying over the sea and thinly populated areas, such as deserts. With this phenomenon in mind a requirement to be subsonic 35nm before the coast was decreed for both acceleration and deceleration. Little mention was made of the 'secondary' or reflected boom that occurs well ahead of the aircraft, depending on temperature and upper wind differences in winter and summer. It only came to my notice when flight trials were taking place from Bahrain where deceleration commenced abeam Dubai, some 180nm distant. My wife observed that she had heard a boom which was not understood at the time. In fact the secondary boom of very low intensity has necessitated a variation of the deceleration point when operating into the USA and Europe. Sonic booms became one of the main criticisms of supersonic transports led by Bo Lundberg, Professor of Aeronautical Research Institute of Sweden.

Noise

Numerous solutions to noise were tried and evaluated during Concorde's development. Correlation of ground tests with flight experience was often

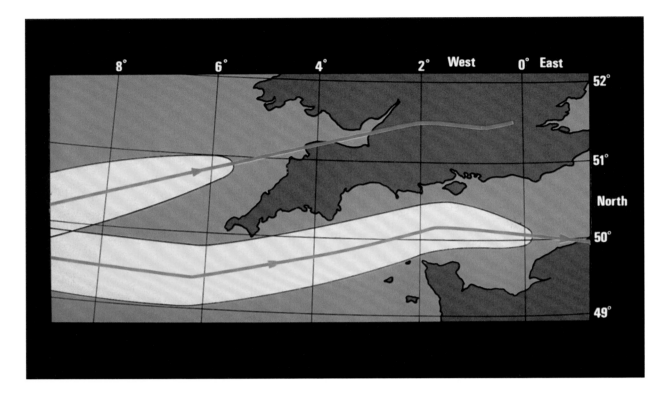

Concorde route patterns for London and Paris. The pale areas show the boom carpet. (BAe Systems)

disappointing when ground-test predictions were not substantiated in flight. Noise became one of the major issues for gaining permission to operate in and out of New York-Kennedy Airport. Much has been written on the subject of Concorde noise, which on the whole is now tolerated world-wide.

A great deal of work went into preparing a detailed presentation of how Concorde operations at New York would work in practice. Some results emanated from flight tests at Casablanca, where a noise abatement technique for Runway 31 Left at Kennedy Airport was developed as the study showed that most departures could use 31 Left or 22 Right. It also showed that the actual noise criteria would be met, especially as the normal take-off weight would be approximately 14 tonnes below maximum. The excellent and precise handling qualities of Concorde gave an exceptional ability to operate in tailwinds and crosswinds and fly tighter patterns than most conventional aircraft, coupled with its high level of performance. Bob McKinlay and Henri Perrier compiled all these facts into a massive document, which was probably the most detailed analysis and study of aircraft noise impact ever made. The advent of large fan engines accentuated Concorde's characteristics, which are still used as a bargaining weapon in trade disputes.

Departure routes for Washington-Dulles, London-Heathrow and Paris-Charles de Gaulle airports were also identified. Concorde flies higher than subsonic jets and consequently gets only a third of the atmospheric shielding from radiation. In order to avoid exposing passengers and crew to excessive radiation, a meter is provided to warn the crew by showing the total of galactic and solar radiation levels. It has never been used in

Left: *The prototype flightdeck showing the weather radar and the gap for the moving map display to be located in the centre panel. (BAe Systems)*

Above: *The Flight Engineer's panels illustrating the large number of dials and switches for the various systems. (BAe Systems)*

Below: *Conventional engine instruments were fitted on the pilot's centre panel on production aircraft. (BAe Systems)*

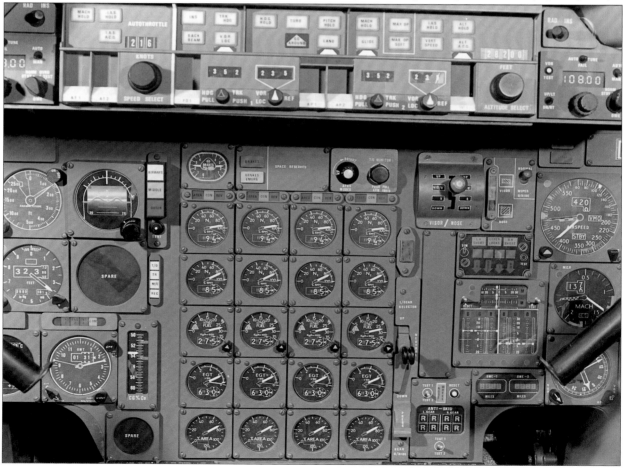

anger except as a media attraction when in the early days it was suggested that only stewardesses beyond child-bearing age should fly as members of the crews, not to mention the males. Concerns about pollution were also raised on occasions, but it is more on future advanced supersonic transports that environmental matters will be a major issue, where every claim good or bad will have to be proven.

The cockpit (flightdeck) is very small and compact. Bringing it to a standard acceptable to the airlines was one of the most time-consuming and frustrating parts of my early involvement in the project. As already mentioned, André Turcat was convinced that a moving map display was essential. It was situated in the middle front panel, taking pride of place with everything else fitting around it. It was a strange philosophy for an aircraft that was going to spend most of its life over the sea. The airlines chucked it out, replacing it with a conventional engine instrument layout using gauges identical to the rest of their fleets. A specially designed auto-monitor instrument that combined all the engine parameters also went down the tube. Meetings with all the option holders in an effort to create a layout for the flight deck was a nightmare but we got there in the end. As mentioned in the chapter entitled Organisation and Responsibilities, TWA were sold on the use of 'strip' instruments, so one layout was produced to satisfy them. The patience and understanding of Doug Vickery, Frank Verrier and Stan Lock was quite amazing.

The prototypes were even more cramped as a navigator's position was included so that the test pilots could concentrate on the job in hand during early development tests. The wearing of protective clothing consisting of pressure helmets and suits, immersion suits, Mae West life-jackets and parachutes was required because the two prototypes were equipped with escape hatches. Their operation at 60,000ft would have produced a cabin altitude of 70,000ft due to the effects of suction. This sort of equipment is alright if it is part of the basic design, but in the case of Concorde it made access to and vision of some switches and controls very difficult. After one or two outings, I disposed of my pressure helmet and reverted to an ordinary 'bone dome' helmet and mask.

A wooden flightdeck mock-up was used for practice emergency escape drills. On one occasion, failure on my part to disconnect some of the equipment attachments practically destroyed the mock-up as I fought towards the escape hatch.

Two other unusual features on the flightdeck were the CG bugs on the mach-meter to show the speed range available for that particular speed, and a CG indicator, which showed the forward and aft limit for the speed. The position of the flying controls is also shown.

John Cochrane, Concorde co-pilot, dressed in full protective clothing. (BAe Systems)

SIMULATORS

Originally, there were two flight-development simulators planned, one to be located at Toulouse and the other at Filton, but the latter was scrapped as an economy measure a year or more before the first flight date predicted in the early plan. Only a fixed-base device usable for specific investigations, e.g. wind shear, existed at Filton. The Toulouse simulator had a three-axis motion system and was tied to the actual flight-control rig. The cockpit layout was prototype standard.

Responsibility for simulation lay in the hands of Sud (later to become Aérospatiale) for handling, while BAe had crew workload studies, which were decreed as part of certification. Many hours were spent in the simulator, which was pessimistic in three areas. First of all there was engine failure at M=1.7, which has already been mentioned; the second was on lateral control on the approach; while the third was engine failure on take-off where the aircraft invariably finished up inverted. This was due to the limitations of the motion system where the effect of yaw was simulated by roll, causing the pilot to boot in the wrong rudder. Consequently, the motion system had to be switched off for take-off assessments.

The crew workload studies were designed to demonstrate that a three-man crew could cope with the task and that the aircraft would fit into normal air traffic and airport procedures. Consequently, various simulated routes were studied, which was a most time-consuming activity.

The simulator was not entirely reliable and was known to run away and jam against the wall of the building where it was situated. A long wait followed, often in somewhat hot and sticky conditions, while a ladder was produced to extract the crew. For all its limitations, excellent work was done to produce the high standard of Concorde's handling characteristics. Jean Pinet, one of the French test pilots, and later head of the training establishment Aéroformation, was in charge of the simulator and regarded it as the bee's knees. His admiration for it was such that when I once asked him if he had enjoyed his first trip in the aircraft, he replied that it was an extension of his simulator experience. It was not one of my favourite pastimes.

There are two flight-training simulators, one at Aéroformation and the other at Filton, comprising a six-axis motion system and visual display. The visual display on the Filton simulator was changed a few years ago from a large apparatus running on rails to a computer-generated device, which has improved its use considerably in teaching landing techniques. The simulator at Filton was originally financed by the Royal Bank of Scotland until BA took it over from them. Plans to move the Filton simulator to Heathrow have always foundered because of worries that

Concorde flight-training simulator located at Filton, showing the runway ahead. (A. Meredith)

putting it all back together might easily fail to provide Concorde flying qualities and negate its CAA approval, so at Filton it remains and the BA crews go there for all basic training and/or route checks. The big difference between a flight-development simulator and a training simulator lies in the fact that the former is based on theoretical data whereas the latter is based on actual parameters measured in flight.

Progress with simulators has been very rapid, so much so that some pilot conversions to a new type are all done on the simulator. The Americans call it 'zero flight time'. Much of this is due to the fantastic visual displays attached to the simulator. The new pilot's first trip in the aircraft is with passengers but accompanied by an instructor pilot. The Filton simulator was not capable of achieving this with its original visual display, which was not adequate for teaching actual landings, so that all landing training was undertaken on a real aircraft. This represented a large number of landings because all the abnormal configurations, i.e. landing with nose/visor up, mechanical flight controls and so on, had to be covered as well as all the landings on four, three or even two engines. The new visual display at Filton is much better and has reduced the number of landings required on an actual aircraft but some still have to be done, mainly because of Concorde's

Concorde flight-training simulator viewed from outside. The six-axis motion system can be clearly seen. (BAe Systems)

rather unusual attitude on landing. The new visual gives the opportunity to fly in and out of New York sky scrapers, which is the greatest fun.

The biggest advantage of flight simulators is that they can be used for 18–20 hours per day and the training cost saving is enormous. There is no limitation on weather to worry about and neither the crew nor the aircraft are put at any risk when carrying out abnormal and emergency procedures. Furthermore, any exercise that is causing any problem to a student can be repeated very easily and quickly.

The flight-development simulator did suffer some deficiencies but it was tremendously valuable as a crew-training tool as well as for sorting out handling characteristics. As mentioned earlier, it is not unusual for the development simulator to be more difficult to 'fly' than the aircraft itself. This was certainly true in the case of Concorde. One particular airline pilot lost his temper completely when subjected to engine failure on the approach in the simulator, but it was after lunch which may account for part of it. The chief aerodynamicist, M. Dequè of Sud, used to spend a great deal of time watching us perform in the simulator and clearly the results meant a lot to him, to whom great credit must go for what turned out to be a beautiful flying machine.

TSS STANDARDS

Safety is the paramount essence of Airworthiness Standards laid down by certification authorities. When a manufacturer applies for certification of an aircraft the relevant certification authority will lay down the requirements against which the aircraft will be assessed. Requirements change and are revised to keep pace with new developments and designs but sometimes this process is not adequate, in which case a list of 'Special Conditions' may be drawn up to cover any item that is not adequately covered or not covered at all. Sometimes a 'Special Condition' may be required for clarification of a particular test.

However, this long-established practice was not considered adequate to meet the case for Supersonic Transports. In fact this applied to Concorde only as there were no other applicants at the time: there were so many new features to be considered and the intended flight operating envelope was to be twice that of subsonic jet transports. The handling characteristics of a slender delta, the wider range of environmental conditions covering temperature changes, turbulence at high speed, the effects of heavy rain, hail, ozone and radiation all had to be considered. Furthermore, adequate speed margins between normal operating speed and maximum design speed had to be demonstrated to show that the high potential energy available at M=2.0 would be contained within the envelope boundaries. Consequently, many new requirements had to be written and some old ones rewritten. A new document called TSS – Transport Super-Sonique – Standards was produced. TSS was to please the French, who place their adjectives arse about face. We would have called it SST. This document both complemented and supplemented the basic airworthiness requirements.

Colin Black of the ARB led the British activity, which was an enormous task running at times in parallel with the aircraft. The first move was to discuss some of the features of a slender delta highlighting the items that might need special attention to ensure that a safety standard comparable to conventional subsonic types was achieved and the method by which this would be assessed. From an aerodynamic point of view consideration of longitudinal characteristics was addressed recognising:

- The lack of a definite stall
- The low lift curve
- Large effect of the elevator
- High-induced drag which means that small departures from the normal speed on initial climb-out had a more pronounced effect than on conventional types
- High inertia in pitch

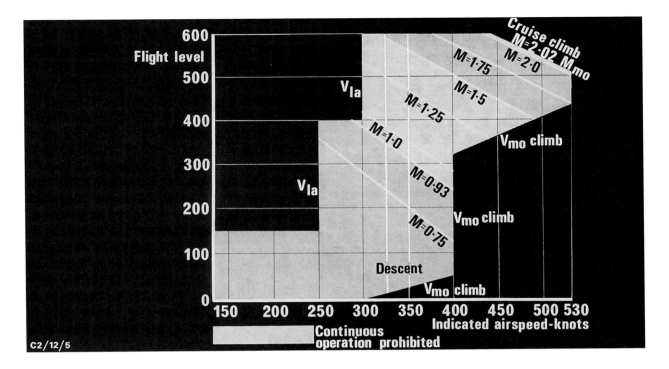

Concorde's flight envelope showing permitted speed/altitude limits for airline use. (BAe Systems)

- Low pitch damping
- The high nose-up attitude at low speed
- The fact that much of the low-speed flight regime was below what is defined as minimum drag speed. This means that descent rate with constant engine power increases as speed is reduced below minimum drag. This is one of the most marked differences between Concorde and conventional aircraft
- The large change in both lift and pitching movement as the aircraft approaches the ground. This is known as 'ground' effect and results in a strong nose-down trim change
- Relatively low wing landing

These were the major items considered. Turning to lateral characteristics, the main focus was on:

- High yaw inertia with respect to roll. This converts angle of attack into sideslip at low speed, which produces adverse yaw
- High level of lateral stability at high angle of attack
- Poor damping in roll
- Distinctive Dutch roll at high angle of attack, Dutch roll being a rolling/yawing motion but in the case of Concorde mainly an oscillation in roll
- The need to use most of the wing trailing edge elevons as ailerons. It was noted that the proximity of the trailing edge to the wing produces proverse yaw

Failure cases covered loss of electrical signalling (i.e. flight controls in mechanical mode) resulting in total absence of auto-stablisation, double engine failures at speeds in excess of M=1.6 and hydraulic malfunctioning, which would cause only half power to be available to the flight-control jacks thus limiting flight control surface angles.

A special feature that needed attention is the movement of the centre of pressure of the wing aft at supersonic speeds. If no action is taken, the aircraft would be flying along with 'up' elevon to counter it, causing excessive drag. Whereas variable camber and twist provide some benefit, the solution is to transfer fuel to match the movement of the centre of pressure. This creates a centre of gravity corridor in which flight operation takes place. A lot of thought was given to the method of indicating this to the crew: a centre of gravity indicator with centre of gravity limits (forward and aft) indicated by moving bugs is provided for the pilots and for the flight engineer. Similar bugs are presented on the machmeters.

Changes had to be made to field-performance requirements for take-off and landing:

- A speed classed as Vmin was used in place of stall speeds Vs or Vms used on conventional types, using take-off power for take-off and approach power for landing
- Rotation speed – VR. This is normally at least 5 per cent above minimum control speed Vmca which is determined in the air following engine failure and 10 per cent above minimum unstick speed. On Concorde the critical speed for successful climb-away was derived from the zero rate of climb speed (Vzrc) rather than from minimum unstick speed (Vmu). Vmca was retained in the formula for calculation

Consequently, a new test for demonstrating lift-off at Vr and climb-away without increasing speed was introduced. Four other abuse cases replaced the conventional engine failure take-off at Vr-5K:

Concorde take-off from London-Heathrow. (BA)

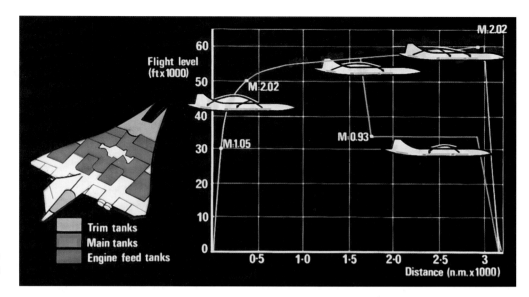

Modes of fuel transfer in a typical supersonic flight. (BAe Systems)

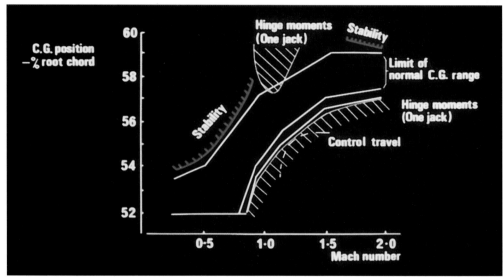

Concorde operates within a centre of gravity corridor dependent on speed. Limitations for aft and forward CG are illustrated. (BAe Systems)

Definition of take-off speeds. Note the introduction of VZRC (Zero Rate of Climb) into the calculation of V2. (BAe Systems)

CASE	SPEED	REQUIREMENT
1	V₁	Deviation not more than 30ft after engine failure from V₁ MIN. to V_LOF. dry runway primary aerodynamic controls only 7Kts. cross wind.
2	V₂	≥ 1·1 V_MCA
3		1 45g available
4		≥ 1·15 V_ZRC Gear up (3 Engines)
5		≥ 1·2 V∝MAX 1g
6		≥ 1·1 V_MIN (3 Engines)
7	V₃	≥ 1·15 V_MCA
8		1·6g Available
9		≥ 1·25 V_ZRC Gear up (All Engines)
10		≥ 1·25 V_MIN Gear up (All Engines)
11	V_R	≥ 1·05 V_MCA
12		Must result in V_LOF ≥ 1·15 V_MU or ≥ 1·1 V_MU if geometry limited
13		No increase in engine cut distance if rotated at V_R - 5 Kts.

a. engine out take-off with all engines rotation rate
b. engine take-off with rotation at 5 per cent less the Vr
c. engine out take-off with a rotation 2 seconds early
d. all engines take-off with rotation 3 seconds late

Compliance required that on all these take-offs the gross flight path from the 35ft screen must not fall below the net flight path (a minimum of 1 per cent less than gross) and that no unsafe characteristics or undue buffeting occur:

- V2 and V3 (i.e. engine out and all engines initial climb speeds) remained referenced to stall or equivalent speed and Vmca, but had to be 1.125 and 1.2 VZRC
- Performance climbs – conventionally WAT (weight, altitude, temperature) climb gradients required to be at least 3 per cent greater than these established in a straight climb or with reduced gradient (2 per cent in a turn). In taking account of the high induced drag and the fact that on Concorde asymmetric flight is carried out with zero sideslip by lowering the wing, a turning technique using 18° bank with all engines operating, 20° bank for one engine out, and 22° for two engines out, was adopted. Take-off climb performance was measured in this way
- Landing – reference speed was established as °

For VTT=1.3Vmin instead of 1.3Vms, but the bonus of a good auto-throttle system enabled this to be reduced to 1.25Vmin. Landing climbs used the same turning flight technique as take-off climbs. Another handling case required the ability to flare from an approach angle of 6° which had to be demonstrated without demanding exceptional skill, or excessive vertical velocity. There were many other aspects in addition which have not been detailed above. The result was that TSS Standards were produced to cover the whole aircraft.

Another unusual aspect of certification was the manner in which the Airworthiness (Certification) Authorities were used to monitor and approve the flight-test programme. The Flight Test Group included representatives from both the British and French airworthiness organisations. The two test pilots in FTG were drawn from this source. The British test pilot, Gordon Corps, was Deputy Chief Test Pilot of the ARB, which led to minor confusion on occasions in terms of which hat he was wearing. While Captain Pierre Dudal, an Air France training captain who was put through the French Test Pilot School, was his French counterpart until he retired, whereupon he was replaced by Captain Gilbert Defer, a French Air Force test pilot who in time joined Aérospatiale and eventually became their chief test pilot.

The policy of using certification pilots to monitor the flight-test programme, and the fact that they participated at various stages in the flight-development programme was strongly opposed by D.P. Davies, Chief Test Pilot of the ARB. He felt that it was fundamentally wrong to mix certification and development. In principle what he felt may well be right, but the arrangement worked quite well in spite of these peculiarities. As a result, Dave Davies rather stood back from flying Concorde, but made selected flights to cover critical cases.

PRE-FIRST FLIGHT PREPARATIONS

A complex project benefits from sustained involvement from the beginning rather than the injection of particular ideas at later stages. By late 1965 when I joined the Concorde programme, the two prototypes were in an advanced state of construction which meant that any changes had a delaying effect and increased costs. Two modifications have already been mentioned in the case of the visor and the flightdeck layout. The runway at Filton was rejected for development flying with some acrimony between the technical directors and myself. Its length was inadequate and there were a number of adverse features such as its slope and sterile areas (a sterile area means that a particular portion cannot be used). At Filton it was the first 1,000ft of the main runway at its eastern end. The fact that the runway was double normal width was totally irrelevant. The issue eventually had to be resolved at a meeting in Sir George Edwards' office. In today's world, the solution would have been to do all the development flying at Toulouse but we were not that far advanced in collaboration to follow such a route. Furthermore, the presence of an assembly line within the UK was part of the reckoning. No one was prepared to agree to what would have been French domination in this field.

Consequently, minds turned towards the British Government's Aircraft & Armament Experimental Establishment (A&AEE) at Boscombe Down. This plan foundered because A&AEE did not want Concorde, based on past experience with the Bristol 188 operation that had taken place there, not to mention its great concern that Concorde would interfere with all A&AEE's normal tasks. Use of the ex-USAF Strategic Air Command base at RAF Fairford came to mind as it was about to be reclassified as a reserve airfield, although still under the auspices of RAF Air Support Command. Its excellent runway was ideal and all the other facilities required could be adapted from that which was available. Permission was granted by the Commander-in-Chief, Air Chief Marshal Sir Thomas Prickett, for the use of Fairford for the development and certification flying. However, this meant the creation of an entirely new task in setting up a total flight-test and maintenance operation with full supporting services without the benefit of previous use before 002 arrived. A great debt is owed to the RAF for its help and co-operation and much credit goes to Eric Hyde, John Dickens and BAC's man on the spot, Wing Commander Tony Pearson, who spearheaded the work on BAC's behalf.

Toulouse did not standstill. A new runway of 13,000ft 150°/330° (15/33) was built in addition to the 9,000ft runway that already existed.

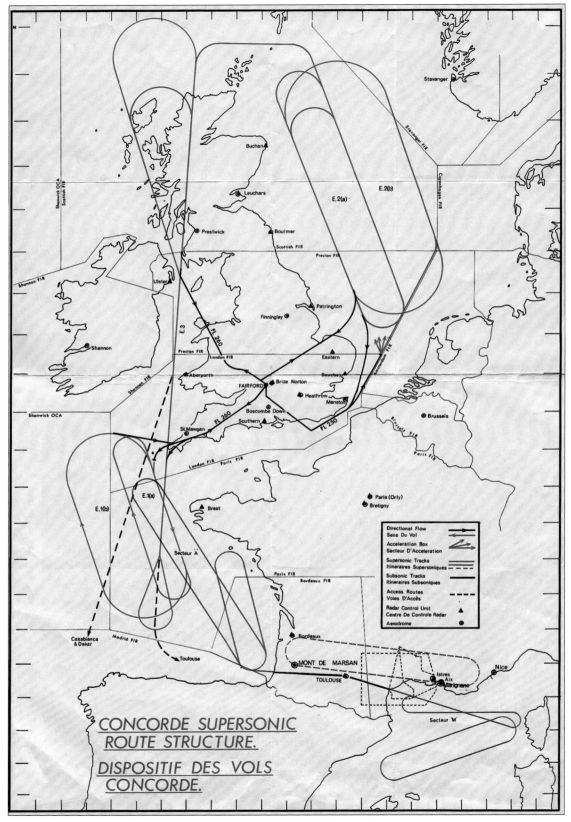

Concorde test routes. (BAe Systems)

An instrument landing system (ILS) was installed at each end, plus a special to Concorde crash barrier at the end of Runway 33. The existing flight hangar was supplemented by a new large assembly hangar. Toulouse never looked back and the present world-class facility of Airbus emanated from Concorde, thus showing the advantages of a government with its sights set on having a major civil-aircraft industry compared to one without any degree of consistency.

Planning of suitable flight test routes both from Fairford and Toulouse and associated procedures were documented in great detail and approved by the Director of Flying, Ministry of Technology and by the Director of the French Flight Test Centre (CEV) at Bretigny. Essentially, full radar coverage had to be available throughout the duration of the flight and a continuous radio link with the respective flight operations rooms at Fairford or Toulouse was specified. In the case of the UK this required the installation of a subsidiary transmitter/receiver radio station situated on a mountain at Craig Owl, Scotland. A triangular course south-west from Toulouse with telemetry coverage was available for 001.

The British Government through the Minister of Technology, Tony Benn, approved a supersonic route over the west coast of Scotland, Wales and Cornwall for high-risk flights with particular emphasis on the ability

HP115 flying at very low speed demonstrates wing vortex bursting from the leading edge of the wing. (BAe Systems)

to find the wreckage, let alone the crew. It was a complicated arrangement requiring prior notification well in advance at 24-hour, 12-hour and 2-hour intervals by which time the aircraft was sometimes unserviceable for flight. However, this did not stop bogus damage claims being made for greenhouse damage and for mink, who kill their young when frightened. The route was not used very much. Normally, all supersonic flights had to take place over the sea. Radar coverage was provided by a combination of British and French radars except in the case of testing from Tangier and Casablanca where there was nothing.

Maintaining flying proficiency while attending all the numerous meetings and learning the aircraft (other than in the company's communication aircraft) had to be addressed and this resulted in a definitive programme organised by the Director of Flying, Ministry of Technology. Apart from flights in the Vulcan Olympus test-bed operated by Rolls-Royce (Bristol Siddeley), flights in a Lightning at the Empire Test Pilot's School (ETPS), a Vulcan Mk2 at B Squadron, Boscombe Down, the BAC221 and HP115 at RAE Bedford were made available to the two lead test pilots in BAC and Sud. In France a Mirage III and a Mirage IV were provided. The precious Mirage IV was actually attached to the Sud flight-test organisation but was destroyed in an accident when flown by the French official pilot. Fortunately, both crew members ejected successfully, suffering only the normal back injuries. A Hunter at RAE Farnborough was also used with inverted spins included in the routine.

Thanks to a close relationship between our Controller of Aircraft (CA), Air Chief Marshal Sir Christopher Hartley and the Commanding General Wright-Patterson Air Force Base, USAF, General Al Boyd, arrangements were made for me to fly 10 hours in a Convair B-58 supersonic bomber on the recommendation of the Officer Commanding Bomber Test Squadron

Mirage IV, attached to the Flight Test Department at Sud Aviation, highlighted the priority afforded to the Concorde project and enabled valuable flight experience at M=2.0 to be attained. (BAe Systems)

Boeing B52 bomber of the US Air Force. The author made a number of flights in this type during a visit to Edwards Air Force Base in 1968. B52s operate from Fairford regularly in times of conflict. (BAe Systems)

The Canberra used as chase for Concorde 002's initial flying. (BAe Systems)

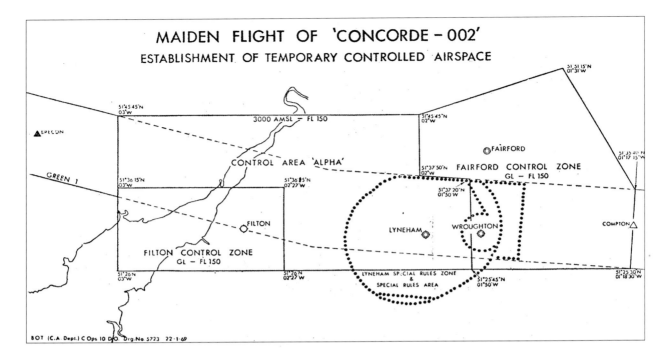

at Edwards Air Force Base, California, Colonel Joe Cotton, an ETPS graduate. This experience was of unique value and four flights were made with Joe Cotton (three) or his deputy Major Ted Stumthal (one). The B-58 carried a crew of three in separate tandem compartments, one behind the other. Vision from the instructor pilot's position was very limited at normal landing speeds of 160–70 knots, so that the recommended technique for landing from the instructor's seat was to increase speed to 225 knots. I tried some of these on one of the flights and considered them to be rather hairy. The whole exercise took one month, because an unscheduled engine change for various defects had to be made after each of the flights in Air Force Jet 662. I filled in the time flying anything available especially the B-52 used for dropping the X-15 and other research vehicles.

The first flights of 001 and 002 were covered by very elaborate arrangements, issued in the form of an operations document in each case. Normal and emergency procedures, location of fire engines and ambulances, operation of the crash barrier and air-traffic-control instructions were included. In the case of 002 even the hospitals to be used were detailed. The 'Statement of Intentions' in the order document for 002 read:

1.1   The purpose of this document is to detail arrangements for the first flight of Concorde 002 (G-BSST) from Bristol (Filton) to Royal Air Force Fairford. It must be appreciated that the procedures detailed are subject to change in respect to experience obtained from 001.

1.2   The Concorde is a civil aircraft and will therefore be operated in accordance with Orders and Regulations contained in the Civil

Aviation Act 1949 including those contained in 'B' conditions approval issued by the Board of Trade. Those orders of AVP67 amended and adjusted as applicable to Concorde will also require compliance.

1.3 Operational and administrative supervision of the test and development flying of British assembled Concorde aircraft is vested in the Director of Flying, Ministry of Technology.

The flight profile was fully detailed, the positioning of the chase aircraft and the coverage of the whole flight under radar were all laid down in specific terms. This document included a large section on crash, rescue and emergency facilities in which every eventuality was described; there was no mention that I can recall of where to take the bodies. RAF Brize Norton was categorised as the diversion airfield.

Special attention was paid to the location of the press and the movement of VIPs, of which there were likely to be many. Public and world-wide interest was very considerable. Toulouse was packed with every form of media and thousands of onlookers, while at Filton nearly all the employees of BAC and Rolls-Royce (about 10–12,000 in all) plus a huge crowd watched from around the airfield. All the roads

Derek John, Sales Director, the late Geoffrey Knight, Chairman of BAC Commercial Aircraft Division, with the author in front of Concorde 002 at RAF Fairford, c. 1973. (BAe Systems)

The Douglas DC-3 Dakota purchased by BAe to shuttle between Filton and Fairford. (BAe Systems)

around Fairford were jammed with onlookers, which necessitated opening a special Concorde car park for subsequent flights. The cost of the car park fell to the Government and no one had the audacity to charge for its use by the public, who had had so much of their money through taxes pumped into the Concorde programme. This did not deter some 'sharp' character one weekend, who arrived in a peaked cap and jerkin adorned with 'National Car Parks' and sporting a bag of tickets for sale. After about 2 hours of relieving onlookers of their pound notes he departed before anyone caught up with him – and with a nice nest egg in his pockets. All efforts to find him failed and he disappeared without trace.

In retrospect it is remarkable that an entirely new facility and organisation could respond so ably and quickly to the demands of Concorde without any practical experience beforehand. It really is a tremendous tribute to those who set it up from scratch. Naturally, there were some problems in the beginning but they were relatively minor. Communication with Filton was given a great deal of attention, as the journey by road took at least 1 hour. I persuaded George Gedge, who had become Managing Director at Filton, to purchase a Douglas DC-3 to supplement the Herons and the Beagle that were available, but which had other duties to perform as well. Public interest in Concorde flights never dwindled during the seven years that we spent at Fairford.

FLIGHT DEVELOPMENT AND CERTIFICATION

GENERAL BACKGROUND

There were three main factors that influenced the length and size of the Flight Development and Certification programme. First, the programme was late. Original targets of a first flight in 1968, followed by entry into service in 1971 were hopelessly optimistic. A review in July 1967 gave a first flight date of February 1968 for 001 and the end of September 1968 for 002, with flight of the first preproduction 01 in January 1970 and the first production 201 in July the same year. The target date for certification was June 1971. When these dates for prototype first flights were obviously going to be missed, in spite of Sud still maintaining February 1968 at the occasion of 001's roll-out in December 1967, the time came when it was essential to get the flight programme under way. Thus, with several of the vital systems missing for full flight-envelope exploration the prototypes were 'half-baked' when they flew but nevertheless were perfectly safe for initial flying.

In an effort to speed up progress on 002, a list of omissions was submitted to me, most of which I rejected (e.g. fitment of one VHF set radio). This exercise was created because of indications that 002 would be ready for its first flight before 001, which in practice was never likely to happen once all parties had agreed to afford all spares priority to 001, but it won a crash barrier for Filton as a precaution. All these deficiencies had to be fitted during planned modification programmes. Furthermore, the change of elevator gearing referred to in the chapter entitled Simulators was considered necessary for flight up to M=2.0 and this took several months on 002 as it involved completely rebuilding the roll/pitch mixing box in the flight-control system.

Secondly, numerous changes had to be made in order to make the Concorde programme a commercially viable proposition. Many changes came about from wind-tunnel and calculated data rather than from actual flight experience. Modifications to the intakes did arise from prototype behaviour, but other changes such as hydraulic-pipe segregation to protect against engine-disc burst were the result of incorrect compliance with airworthiness requirements. The engine starting systems gave some headaches in that the prototypes were equipped with Gas Turbine Starters (GTS) on

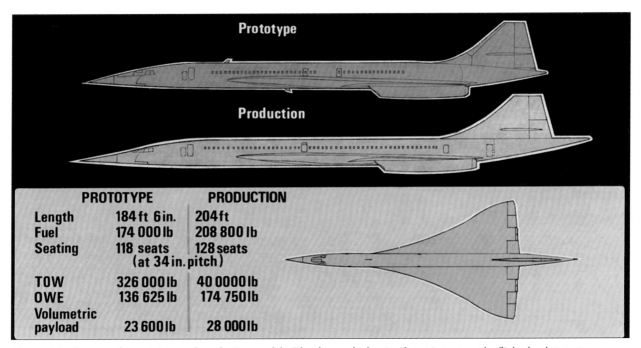

	PROTOTYPE	PRODUCTION
Length	184 ft 6 in.	204 ft
Fuel	174 000 lb	208 800 lb
Seating	118 seats	128 seats
	(at 34 in. pitch)	
TOW	326 000 lb	40 0000 lb
OWE	136 625 lb	174 750 lb
Volumetric payload	23 600 lb	28 000 lb

Comparision between the prototype and production models. The changes had a significant impact on the flight development programme. These changes were necessary to make Concorde commercially viable. Extra cost and delays in the flight-test programme resulted. (BAe Systems)

Concorde 002 ground running with the detuner silencers at Filton prior to first flight. Baffle fences can also be seen. (BAe Systems)

Concorde 001 at the roll-out ceremony at Toulouse in December 1967. (BAe Systems)

André Turcat and the author on the flightdeck of Concorde 001 at Toulouse during the initial taxi test. (BAe Systems)

engines 2 and 4, which seemed a good idea because the GTS could drive the engine's auxiliary gear box, thus achieving electric and hydraulic power on the ground. However, if the GTS failed, there was no other way to start that particular engine. A wild alternative appeared on the preproduction 01 using a hydrazine fuel device for emergency generation. Hydrazine fuel requires special precautions for personnel handling it and appeared to be generally nasty, so how it was conceived for world-wide use on a civil transport escapes comprehension. In the end a conventional air start system from a truck and a ram air turbine for emergency hydraulic power were installed.

The differences between the prototype, preproduction and the production aircraft were so significant that the prototypes really became vehicles for proof of concept in terms of certification. This did not affect the task of demonstrating sustained M=2.0 capability, but what did result however was the need to conduct several critical programmes such as in-flight flutter many times over.

The flight trials programme was supposed to reflect the design responsibilities of BAC and Sud, but a more flexible disposition of tasks allocated to each development aircraft occurred in practice. However, the basic responsibilities of handling and aerodynamics by Aérospatiale, and performance and powerplant by BAC remained intact.

Configuration differences and a special requirement to carry out 1,000 hours of route-proving/endurance flying combined to make Concorde's flight-trials programme the largest test task to date. It amounted to approximately 5,500 hours lasting nearly seven years.

Thirdly, and of great significance, Concorde was a new venture with a flight envelope twice that of a subsonic aircraft and with a new set of airworthiness requirements, which in certain cases were still being written.

FIRST FLIGHT OF PROTOTYPES

Prior to flight, all the engine ground running and systems testing were carried out by the flight crews of each prototype. Consequently, the crews' knowledge of the whole aircraft was very extensive. Ground-running bases with large detuners and baffle fences were constructed at Filton, Fairford and Toulouse. In addition an underground bunker equipped with closed-circuit television was built at Filton. I accompanied André Turcat on 001's first taxi tests in August 1968, though we had already decided that high-risk flights would not be flown by mixed crews.

The Russian Tu144 stole the date of a first flight of a civil supersonic transport on 31 December 1968, but 001 followed soon afterwards on 2 March 1969, with André Turcat at the controls. Two days of poor weather had postponed 001's first flight due to a tailwind and mist, but on the third day visibility had improved sufficiently (although there was still a tail wind) for Turcat and 001 to lift off from Runway 33 at Toulouse. This particular runway was chosen because of the crash barrier installed at one end. The crew was as follows:

André Turcat – Captain
Jacques Guiguard – Co-pilot

Tu144 with nose drooped and canard fore-plane prominent. (BAe Systems)

Michel Retief – Flight Engineer
Henri Perrier – Chief Flight Test Observer
Claude Durand – Flight Observer
Jean Belon – Assistant Chief of Flight Test, SNECMA

Jacques Guiguard retired soon after the first flight for health reasons and Henri Perrier would later go on to succeed André Turcat as Director of Flight Test.

The flight lasted for 42 minutes and covered general handling and pilot's assessment up to 10,000ft and 250k, before 001 came in for a perfect landing by André Turcat in spite of the tail-wind component. The beauty of Concorde in flight captured the whole of the aviation world and was a thrilling sight. Eight more flights were made in March 1969 with speed and altitude increased to 350k and 30,000ft. Flight 5 was flown by me at André Turcat's generous invitation, thus providing valuable experience for flying 002 on 9 April 1969.

Behind the scenes, apparently there had been a major problem brewing over hotel accommodation for the hundreds of press who had gathered at Toulouse. This resulted in several close discussions between André Turcat and General Ziegler, head of Aérospatiale, before a decision to fly was announced. Publicity has its place, but mixed up with a first flight is not one of them.

A different form of frustration surrounded the first flight of 002. Two attempts to complete the final taxi test up to 120k were abortive because the failure flag on the captain's airspeed indicator operated at 100K on each occasion and could not be ignored, although the instrument appeared to be working correctly. 002 was cleared for flight prior to each high-speed taxi test, so on the third attempt, with all the experts convinced

Concorde 002 about to push back at Toulouse, May 1971. (BAe Systems)

that the defect had been fixed, I decided that I would continue into flight if it worked. This is what happened. 002's second flight was held up for two days while I recovered from a badly cut hand, thanks to a saw, as Director of Flying would not clear anyone else to fly as captain/first pilot until further flying had taken place.

PHASE 1 – TESTING

001's main task was to expand the permitted flight envelope in speed and altitude. This was progressed by an extensive in-flight flutter programme which is aimed to demonstrate that any induced oscillations damp out, thus showing positive structural damping. This is done by applying rapid movements of the flight control surfaces by artificial means followed by immediate release. The length of time it takes the resulting oscillation to damp out is recorded as well as other structural vibrations. Ensuring 'the tail does not wag the dog' is commonly used to describe flutter testing. Concorde test aircraft were fitted with small rocket packs on the control surfaces known as 'bonkers' and an out-of-balance exciter monitor was installed in the hydraulic systems enabling excitation to be involved over the whole structural frequency range. The third device was an electronic stick jerk box which controlled the 'jerk' input very accurately and consistently, whereas jerks induced by the pilot often vary. Special attention was needed to the transonic portion of the flight envelope and the number of test points were more concentrated. Furthermore, as an additional precaution the two rudders were bolted together on the prototype. There were no incidents during any of the flutter programmes.

002 covered many performance and handling tests including handling without auto-stabilisation, engine relights, flight in heavy rain and on a wet runway and three-engine and two-engine overshoots. A slight interruption came when it was decided that both prototypes would display at the Paris (Le Bourget) Salon on 8 and 9 June 1969. 001 was

Concorde 001 on its maiden take-off at Toulouse, 2 March 1969. (BAe Systems)

Sir George Edwards was the first non-member of Flight Test to fly in Concorde. He is seen emerging from 002 at Fairford at the end of a test flight flown by André Turcat with the author as co-pilot, 30 July 1969. (BAe Systems)

A special test route over Scotland, Wales and south-west England was established for initial flights at M=2.0. (BAe Systems)

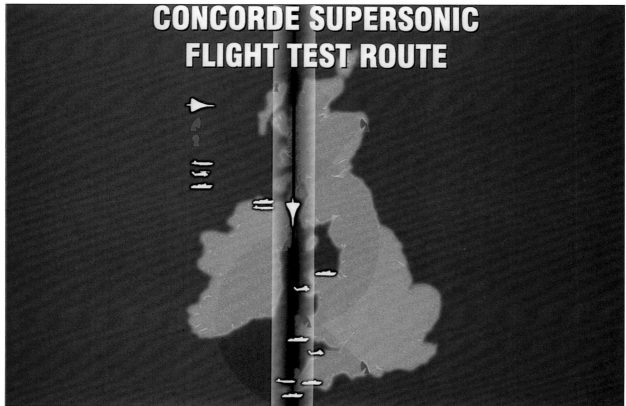

CONCORDE SUPERSONIC
FLIGHT TEST ROUTE

positioned at Le Bourget for the whole show, during which a number of VIPs, especially airline presidents, flew in the aircraft. 002 operated from Fairford on both days and performed a co-ordinated display with 001, albeit unrehearsed, which received a tremendous accolade.

Just before Paris, 001 was flown by a mixed Sud/FTG crew in order to get approval from CDV for the flying display at Le Bourget. Gordon Corps similarly flew 002 at Fairford for general assessment purposes at speeds up to M=0.8 and 30,000ft, with special attention to flight and approach in mechanical signalling mode of the flight controls. 002 took part in the Queen's Birthday flypast over Buckingham Palace, flying right over the flagpole, thanks to London radar.

We had all decided by this time that we did not like the 17½° nose position for landing, as there was nothing in front of the pilot's eyes and there was a feeling of looking over a precipice. Consequently, the 17½° nose position was modified to 12½° for fully down.

Flight test progress was conveyed to all the airlines through Concorde *Flight News*, produced by the BAC-Sud Joint Sales Organisation. These now make very interesting reminders of what went on, although personally I have a complete record of every flight made by British development aircraft. In any event, constraints of space make it impractical to include all this information here, which tends to be repetitive anyway.

At the end of July 1969, 002 commenced a major grounding in order to incorporate a new flight-control system mixing box in order to provide a change of gearing of the inner elevons and a fully operational intake control system. André Turcat, accompanied by myself and Sir George Edwards, the first non-member of Flight Test to fly in Concorde, carried out two flights on 002 for comparative purposes on the day before the grounding. The work programme included fitment of an Inertial Navigation System, installation of Olympus 3-B engines, different radio altimeters and a general up-date. The elevon gearing change arose from simulator tests where the failure of an outer engine at M=1.7 produced excessive roll and sideslip which made the aircraft almost uncontrollable. 002 gearing was changed from a 1:1 gearing, which set up a large side force on the fin, to 0.3:1 roll to pitch. This was more than necessary and production aircraft were set at 0.7:1. 001 was never modified because actual flight results showed that the problem could be handled with experience, although this was still unacceptable for airline service. The grounding of 002 was completed on 20th March 1970.

In the meantime 001 was prepared for the initial supersonic phase having opened up the flight envelope to 410k and a Mach number M=0.85, continued with 380k and M=0.9 and 330k and M=0.95. The combined block time for the subsonic phase was 103hrs 48mins.

PHASE TO M=2.0

Concorde 001 flew at supersonic speed for the first time on 1 October 1969 up to M=1.05 where handling checks, simulated engine failure and with auto-stabilisation off were evaluated. Movement of the centre of gravity in flight by fuel transfer covered the range of 51.1 per cent to 57.4 per cent. The 'barn-door' intakes, as they were known, incorporated an auxiliary door on the underside of each intake. For take-off, the door opened outwards in order to supply additional air and was hinged at the rear. During subsonic climb or cruise, the door-hinge arrangement changed automatically to the front, so that the door could then operate in a spill mode in the event of engine failure. This was a flawed concept because failure to change automatically from rear-hinge position to front hinge prohibited flight at supersonic speeds. In other words, one was entirely dependent on the automatic change-over. It was only a question of time before it was not hinged at either end but, fortunately, this happened in the hangar and the door fell on the floor as a result. This arrangement was changed without too much debate.

A significant milestone was achieved in November 1969 when airline Captains James Andrew (BOAC), Paul Roitsch (Pan Am), Maurice Bernard (Air France) and Vernon Laursen (TWA), accompanied by flight engineers John Lidiard (BA), John Anderson (Pan Am), Martial Detienne (Air France) and Eugene Manning (TWA), flew 001 at Toulouse in a series of evaluation flights. Their report read: 'For all the flight conditions flown during this phase, the aircraft was pleasant and easy to fly, imposed no excessive workload on the pilot even in failure conditions, and there should be no problem in training airline pilots and engineers to handle the aircraft.'

The author, John Cochrane, Brian Watts, Roy Lockhart, John Allan, Mike Addley and Peter Holding boarding 002 dressed in protective flying kit prior to a test flight, c. 1969. (BAe Systems)

Damage to the intakes on 001 following heavy engine surge when the front ramp and operating mechanism failed in No. 4 intake in 1971. Some of the subsequent debris also affected No. 3 intake too. (BAe Systems)

View of the front ramps. (Jonathan Falconer)

Further flutter flights increased speed to M=1.5/500k (1,000mph). This flying was all done with fixed intake ramps and demonstrated that M=1.5 was the maximum speed attainable in this condition and furthermore that a spill facility was required for engine failure in order to avoid excessive buffet. Captain Pierre Dudal of CEV flew 001 three times up to this point and reported: 'For a prototype of such complexity, the first impression is of remarkable "availability" which is comparable to present commercial aircraft. All systems function satisfactorily and the engines have never caused any major difficulties. One flight only was delayed because of engine starting.'

Sonic boom measurements were also made and the use of in-flight reverse for rapid descent was also determined as standard procedure. Progress of flight tests can be summarised as: 100 hours in 5 months, 100 flights in 9 months, 200 hours in 10 months, supersonic in 7 months, 1,000mph in 9 months.

002 re-appeared in March 1970 with revised elevon gearing, Olympus 593-3B engines, fully operable intake system and flutter excitation installation, so that it could take over speed increases to M=2.0. In the meantime 001 was grounded for fitment of the move-able intake system and other updating, with the exception of the elevon gearing change. By September 1970, 002 had progressed to M=1.7 and successfully completed double engine failures, which were entirely docile. Five appearances were made at the SBAC Air Show, Farnborough, and on the last of these we diverted to London Heathrow due to inclement weather at Fairford, landing above maximum landing weight and making a lot of noise in the process at constant speed approach, which was normal practice in the early days. A very light take-off out of Heathrow, which put the aircraft at over 2,500ft at the end of the runway, made some amends. Later on we used a technique of decelerating from 210k at 800ft to target threshold speed. This was modified by British Airways to 190K at 800ft.

An interesting incident took place when the Minister of Aviation, Tony Benn, came on a flight soon after the grounding period. The test called for flight with one hydraulic system switched off, known as flying on 'half bodies'. On switching off one system, the aircraft developed an uncontrollable gentle roll, necessitating switching back to both systems very quickly. After-flight investigation showed that the power control units had a dormant fault in one of the valves which allowed this to happen. This was a basic design fault which took about three months to fix, during which time both aircraft were grounded.

By November 1970, the stage was set to achieve M=2.0. André Turcat and myself decided that 002 should lead because of the elevon gearing modification. We routed out to the North Sea via the Wash for acceleration and final run down the special west-coast route (boom-alley). The first attempt was thwarted by a false fire warning on No. 2 engine and a second five days later by an oil leak on No. 4 engine. 001 was rearing to go as the engine failure case at M=1.7 was nothing like as bad as the simulator suggested and so André Turcat achieved M=2.0 immediately after 002's abortive attempt. Anyway, third time lucky for 002 on 12 November 1970, achieving M=2.0 at 50,300ft. Travelling at 20nm per minute mopped up the west-coast route pretty quickly but time on test was sufficient. Abeam South Wales, I asked John Cochrane to throttle the engines and then the fun began. We thought that World War Three had started as engines 3 and 4 went into what is called cyclic surge (a series of continuing surges). There were about seven interactive surges between engines 3 and 4, but without any previous experience of engine surge on Concorde this came as a big surprise. Reduction of speed eventually stopped the surging and a somewhat chastened return to Fairford followed. Clearly, this would not do and a series of flights where surges were deliberately induced followed. Normally, the induced surge was preceded by rough running, as the technique was to move manually either ramp or spill door or both off schedule, but it was still unpleasant when it occurred.

Achievement of sustained flight at M=2.0 was a major milestone and gave an enormous boost to everyone concerned. An aft centre of gravity of 58.5 per cent and flight at combined mmo/vmo 2.0/530k had been demonstrated with various forms of simulated failure, e.g. engines.

Fortuitously, both prototypes were fitted with petal-type speed brakes on the rear fuselage and these were used to decelerate from M=2.0 to M=1.7 where normal engine throttling was followed. The prototypes operated in this manner throughout the remainder of their test programmes because of engine surge when throttling at M=2.0.

A major incident occurred on 001 in January 1971, when the aircraft, flying at M=1.98 with reheats running on engines 1 and 3, experienced an engine overspeed on cutting reheat on No. 3 engine, which entered heavy surge and interacted into No. 4 engine. The intensity of the surge in No. 4 led to the failure of the forward intake drive coupling, thence to failure of the two actuating links and of the hinge at the ramp's leading edge. Thus No. 4 ramp was spat out, damaging the lower lip of the intake and various bits of metal were ingested by both engines 3 and 4. The test pilot,

Gilbert Defer, had no trouble controlling the aircraft but the large number of warning lights and gongs, which the French were very keen on, caused some confusion. The aircraft returned to Toulouse without further difficulties. As a result, massive strengthening of the ramp mechanism and a change to the intake control-system law was made. The number of lights and warnings were also reduced.

Attention to the high-speed envelope was not the only activity. Performance was covered in great detail and improved sealing of the nacelles was carried out to improve it. The low-speed regime was investigated very fully by 001. Concorde does not stall in the traditional sense but develops a very high sink rate as angle of attack is increased. At the minimum demonstrated speed of 119k with take-off power applied, a descent rate of about 7,000ft/min with wings level was reached with an angle of attack of 28°, where directional and lateral control became very marginal. This was no great surprise because wind-tunnel and free model tests had indicated that above 23° directional stability and elevon effectiveness would be reduced due to changes in the wing vortex pattern. Consequently, two anti-stall systems are provided in order to protect against this rather unlikely situation and to demonstrate compliance with the airworthiness regulations. (A full description of the system is given in Appendix VII.)

A further deficiency in relation to airworthiness requirements was longitudinal stability – a complicated subject, but simply defined it is an aircraft's tendency to return to its original attitude if disturbed from a trimmed state. In order words, a pull force to reduce speed and a push force to increase speed should be required. Concorde was neutrally stable up to M=0.95, when it became unstable to M=1.3 and then neutrally stable up to M=2.0. This meant that there was virtually no trim change over the whole speed range. It was therefore necessary to fit an automatic mach trim system in order to show compliance with airworthiness requirements for all civil aircraft (this is a military requirement as well). This was a pity as the prototypes were more pleasant to fly than later models, which had the system fitted.

View of Concorde elevon.
(Jonathan Falconer)

PROGRAMME EXPANSION AND FIRST EXPOSURES

Following the intake incident on 001, the whole intake structure and operating mechanisms were beefed up considerably. 002 spent several flights measuring loads imposed by induced surges of which more than 100 were made. The time had now arrived when a lot of senior VIPs wanted to sample Concorde and there was a general need to show it to the world as a counter to the constant threat hanging over the project. Furthermore, tests away from base had to take place in order to cover tropical, high-altitude and cold-soak conditions for both performance measurements and systems.

Sustained flight at M=2.0 by both prototypes was a major milestone in its own right and demonstrated proof of concept, but it also showed the size and scope of the task remaining to produce a commercially viable transport, albeit with the assistance of the later development aircraft, which were beginning to appear on the horizon. Much of the early flying had been hand flown, although auto-pilot tests and automatic landings

The author escorting HRH Prince Bernhard of the Netherlands down the steps from 002 followed by HRH Prince Philip Duke of Edinburgh and Sir George Edwards following a ground inspection of the aircraft, January 1972. (BAe Systems)

had started. This showed the very precise handling characteristics of Concorde throughout all the phases of flight. Some degradation in mechanical mode, especially on approach and landing, had been noted but considered acceptable for an emergency condition.

In May 1971, President Georges Pompidou flew from Paris-Le Bourget to Toulouse with a prolonged supersonic cruise over the Bay of Biscay in 001. 002 was positioned at Toulouse to meet him. This was followed by the first intercontinental flight from Toulouse to Dakar, returning direct to Paris-Le Bourget for the Paris Air Show. A number of VIPs, particularly airline presidents, and French, British and American journalists, all flew in 001. President Pompidou flew to the Azores later in the year to meet President Nixon and by now the use of a Concorde for French presidential trips overseas became standard procedure. A tour of South America by 001 lasting two weeks was very successfully completed. Meanwhile, HRH Prince Philip and

Edouard Elyan, Chief Test Pilot for the Tu144, and the author on the flightdeck of 002 at the Hanover Air Show, April 1972.
(BAe Systems)

HRH Prince Bernhard flew 002 at M=2.0 during a test flight. BOAC came in force at chairman and board level along with Lord Rothschild and his 'Think tank', followed by HRH Princess Margaret and Prime Minister Edward Heath. These types of flights may appear as time wasting but this was not the case. It was always possible to do some test and any added knowledge was of great value.

002's first operation away from base was attendance at the Hanover Air Show, accompanied by Michael Heseltine, Minister of Aviation. The arrival of the Tu144 prototype just ahead of Concorde rather upset the apple cart by scraping all its exhaust nozzles on landing and frightening the air-show organisers to the extent that neither of us was allowed to fly. The length of runway at Hanover was slightly short for the prototypes but Concorde had no problem stopping well within the distance available. Advantage was taken of the enforced two-day period on the ground to change a GTS on 002 and to spend the rest of the time examining the Tu144 and vice-versa. The Russian co-pilot spoke English very well with a strong American accent; sadly he was killed when the Tu144 crashed at Paris. We all got on extremely well, but found some elements of the Tu144 combined aspects of a modern civil transport and a Second World War bomber. The Russians

The tail bumper on Concorde incorporates a small wheel in order to avoid sparks if contact with the runway occurs during landing. (BAe Systems)

The first preproduction Concorde 01 G-AXDN in flight, 17 December 1971. Note the absence of a rear fuselage extension. (BAe Systems)

showed particular interest in some of the Concorde flightdeck instruments, which we had in fact decided to ditch on later models.

In June 1972, 002 commenced a most ambitious tour of the Middle and Far East, Japan and Australia. Admittedly, it was very well supported by maintenance and technical staff who were carried in a RAF VC10 together with a spare engine in a Short Belfast also of the RAF. A great deal of vital information was gained from this trip, the full itinerary of which is given in Appendix X.

First stop was Athens where the take-off for Teheran was nothing short of frightening. Concorde did not relish the bumps and undulations of the runaway, which caused violent oscillations of the fuselage and flightdeck in particular. The pilots' headsets came off and I was shouting at the other pilot, Johnnie Walker, who was flying, to keep going in case he aborted the take-off at too late a stage. This feature actually remained for the rest of the trip, especially at Bangkok and Singapore. At Teheran the thermal plugs in the tyres blew necessitating a wheel change, which prompted the Shah's personal bodyguard to demand an air test. This I refused and won the argument in exchange for a Concorde tie, pen – and nearly one's shirt.

The Shah flew next day and I was strapping him into the left-hand seat at M=2.0, when a large drop in outside air temperature occurred. The auto-pilot could not compete with the change and commenced a rapid climb followed by an even more rapid descent during which air speed rose to 550k, 20k above the normal limit. Subsequent investigation showed that the degree of temperature shear was near to prediction but that it occurred over a much shorter horizontal distance than had been assumed. However, the Shah was well pleased and indicated that Iran Air would purchase three Concordes following normal negotiations. Landing at Bombay outbound was peculiar because thousands of onlookers had broken lines and were jammed along each side of the runway. It was like landing on a football pitch.

The next lesson was learnt between Bombay and Bangkok. Concorde was predicted to fly above the weather in cloudless skies but this was not to be since a major storm was positioned over the Bay of Bengal, so

Concordes 001 and 02, nearest the camera, at Toulouse. The transparent visor on 02 is seen. (BAe Systems)

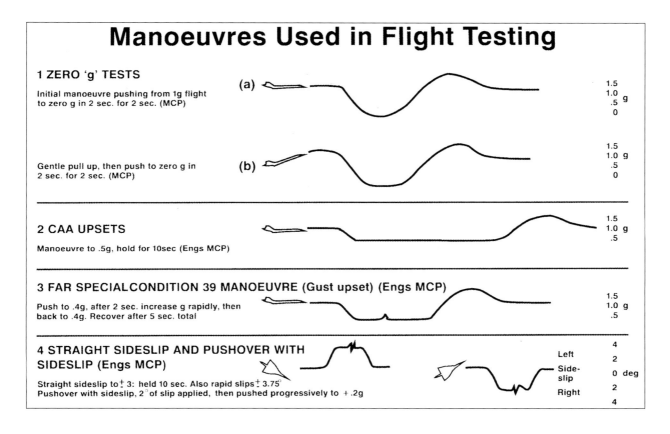

Manoeuvres Used in Flight Testing

1 ZERO 'g' TESTS

Initial manoeuvre pushing from 1g flight to zero g in 2 sec. for 2 sec. (MCP)

(a)

1.5
1.0 g
.5
0

Gentle pull up, then push to zero g in 2 sec. for 2 sec. (MCP)

(b)

1.5
1.0 g
.5
0

2 CAA UPSETS

Manoeuvre to .5g, hold for 10sec (Engs MCP)

1.5
1.0 g
.5

3 FAR SPECIAL CONDITION 39 MANOEUVRE (Gust upset) (Engs MCP)

Push to .4g, after 2 sec. increase g rapidly, then back to .4g. Recover after 5 sec. total

1.5
1.0 g
.5

4 STRAIGHT SIDESLIP AND PUSHOVER WITH SIDESLIP (Engs MCP)

Straight sideslip to ± 3: held 10 sec. Also rapid slips ± 3.75°
Pushover with sideslip, 2° of slip applied, then pushed progressively to + .2g

Left 4
2
Side-slip 0 deg
Right 2
4

Concorde was in a cloud at 60,000ft with tops going well above. Further temperature shears showed up the inadequacy of the auto-pilot to keep the aircraft within permitted speed limits.

It was normal practice for overseas trips to be accompanied by a Government minister, Michael Heseltine and his wife covered the first part of the tour and were replaced at Singapore by Lord and Lady Jellicoe. Mrs Heseltine became extremely poorly between Bombay and Bangkok but fortunately the services of Fred Clauson, a BOAC steward, saved the day with some oxygen in the decidedly primitive passenger cabin.

Noise and smoke at Tokyo did not go down too well but landing in one direction and taking off in the opposite direction gave some alleviation on demonstration flights and on departure to Manila. Darwin produced the first bomb scare for Concorde from a mysterious telephone call in the middle of the night. As is so often the case, it was a complete hoax. A rapturous welcome occurred at Sydney, although the airfield fire brigade got rather excited when the tail bumper (fitted to prototypes) touched the runway and threw up a few sparks, which was perfectly normal. However, it encouraged a decision to fit a small wheel on the bumper of production aircraft. Visits to Melbourne and Adelaide all went very well with good serviceability and schedule keeping. The return part of the trip posed one particular problem on the Bangkok–Bombay sector where the only suitable alternative was Delhi. Fuel reserves were such that any decision to divert to Delhi had to be made before descent through 25,000ft. At this point the weather at Bombay was declared as wide open. However, at about 20 miles from Bombay with the aircraft now committed, it

Actual flight traces taken from flight-test recordings. (BAe Systems)

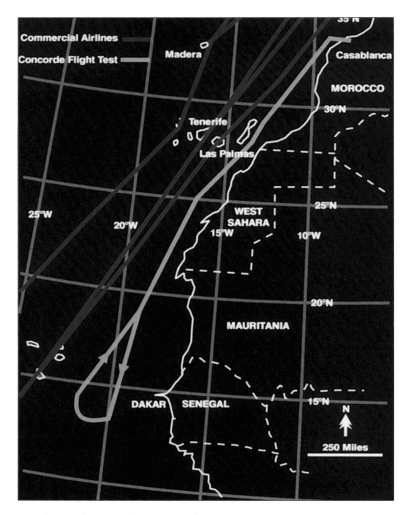

In order to achieve very low ambient temperatures for engine intake development test flights were made from Tangier and Casablanca. There was no radar coverage on the southerly test route. (BAe Systems)

was quite obvious that the monsoon had arrived with a vengeance. 002 then entered cloud and we broke out at 400ft in very heavy rain, which made stopping after landing quite difficult but thanks to the tail parachute and reverse thrust there was plenty of runway left. A Boeing 707 following was not quite so lucky and went off the end.

All this convinced me to chicken out of a planned demonstration flight and unserviceability was declared. This was the only flight including demonstrations at Teheran, Singapore (3), Tokyo (2), Sydney (1), Melbourne (1), Darwin (1), Dhahran (1) and Beirut (1) that was not completed to schedule. Heathrow was reached after a stopover at Toulouse with the Concorde 'antis' in full cry, although their efforts were somewhat spoilt by specially prepared postcards drawing attention to noise being posted 24 hours before we arrived.

In the month, 002 had completed approximately 70 hours' block time, 60 hours' flight time from which two particular deficiencies required urgent attention. First, the auto-pilot needed to be improved considerably. This took a long time, the details of which will be covered later. Secondly, the aircraft response to rough runways was not acceptable, although the French took some convincing. André Turcat and I went back to Athens. After one take-off in 001, I said to him, 'there you are, unacceptable', to which Turcat replied 'I would not agree unacceptable, but it might interfere with emergency procedures'. Anyway, modification did eventually appear in the form of a two-stage oleo but introduction was after airline service commenced. Consequently, runways to be used had to be cleared individually at the start of service. The modification was proven at Gander and finally included take-offs on Runway 31 Left at New York-Kennedy. The runway at Singapore was re-laid at British Government expense to enable Concorde to operate there.

TOWARDS THE FINAL GOAL

Concorde 01 came on the scene following extensive engine and systems checks on the ground and a full ground resonance structural programme had been completed, reflecting the major differences between preproduction and prototype. All of this took more than one month, including taxi tests, and first flight took place on 17 December 1971. This flight from Filton to Fairford was curtailed when the landing gear commenced cycling up and down after the first selection of 'up'. In its first phase, 01 carried out flutter, handling, performance and water-ingestion tests. The decision to change the intake control system to a digital system had been taken by this time and so the aircraft flew without an AICS which limited it to M=1.5 for nine months after which time it went back to Filton until March 1973 for a total update and the fitment of the new AICS.

Meanwhile, the two prototypes continued their programmes of handling, intake investigations and performance with VIP flights introduced fairly regularly. I took 002 to Johannesburg for hot and high performance trials routing Las Palmas, Robertsfield and Luanda. It had become normal practice to fly the country's national flag on arrival but unfortunately our sales organisation had made a gross misjudgement because we flew the rebel flag at Luanda. The authorities were not pleased and threatened jail for the crew. They eventually understood that the mistake was genuine but were even more put out when the correct flag was not flown prior to take-off. No flags on departure was our normal practice because the flag required the direct vision (DV) window to be opened. Soldiers with 'pop' guns surrounded 002 at the take-off point, so

HRH Princess Anne speaking to Charlie Andrews, Maintenance Manager at Fairford, before flying in 002, 23 October 1973. (BAe Systems)

that a return to the apron was the only option before further explanations were made and take-off was permitted. British crews used to wear orange overalls following American practice, as the colour had been shown to be advantageous to search and rescue operations, but we discovered that all the loo cleaners at Johannesburg also wore the same colour.

The performance trials programme consisted of measured take-offs, with and without simulated engine failure, climb performance and measured landings including threshold speed (VTT) – 5k on the forward centre of gravity limit, which was the test that had proved very difficult on some aircraft in the past, but Concorde proved very easy, even at VTT–10k. Gordon Corps of the CAA did quite a lot of the flying in South Africa as part of the FTG's involvement. VIP flights, including one for the Prime Minister of South Africa, took place from Cape Town.

02 joined the programme and once again new features such as the extended rear fuselage, the TRA nozzle and carbon brakes appeared for the first time. Although 02 was still not fully representative of the production model, one had the feeling that we were getting there, albeit rather slowly. Despite the fact that 01's contribution to the programme overall was considerable, an attempt was made at official level to pull the aircraft out of the programme, but the manufacturers managed to scotch the idea. When it returned from Filton in March 1973, the 01's flight envelope had been rapidly expanded and the major task of proving the air-intake control system began in earnest.

For certification purposes a speed of M=2.18 was required for clearance of M=2.05 cruise (later changed to 2.04) under TSS requirements, although initial thoughts believed M=2.21 was needed. In fact M=2.23 was achieved on 01 and M=2.21 on production aircraft 202 subsequently.

A temperature spectrum of ISA + 12°C to ISA -30°C was considered to be adequate for demonstrating the full capability of the system. While the temperature conditions at the high end could be covered from Fairford, this was not the case for the low temperature condition, which was in fact the critical case. Surges in level flight over the whole speed envelope using ramp/spill door inching was the method to induce surge. Engine Nos 1 and 2 on aircraft 01 were strain-gauged, so engines 1 and 2 became the test engines. This had one major disadvantage in that No. 1 engine supplied the air conditioning to the flightdeck and engine surge filled the flightdeck with a very unpleasant acrolein gas. Several crew members reported sore throats and a local vacuum company, which no doubt made a fortune, had to be called in on a regular basis to clean out the system. Fortuitously, further experience showed No. 4 engine to be the critical case, and so Nos 3 and 4 became the test engines. It was immediately appreciated that to conduct tests in the peripheral envelope, the influence of the N1/N2 limiter had to be removed and the flight engineer was provided with a limited manual control of N1, so that one pair of engines could be operated at lower N1, thus giving an increased surge margin. On the two excursions mentioned previously, to speed in excess of M=2.2, the N1 had been wound down to the extent that the aircraft would not go any faster.

It is as well that an early decision to produce a M=2.05 vehicle and not a M=2.2 one, as was originally intended, was indeed made. I am not sure how it could ever have been achieved without extensive modification. It was the structural temperature reduction which improved fatigue life that brought the change in the first place. Cruise at M=2.2 would have required demonstration at M=2.35.

02 may not have been fully representative of production but it looked like the finished article, particularly with the rear fuselage extension, which contributed significantly to Concorde's beauty. Carbon brakes were installed for the first time on a Concorde and, although they required some initial development, their use on Concorde was the foundation for their eventual widespread use on civil aircraft. 02 was assigned to a cold-soak programme at Anchorage, Alaska, as one of its primary tasks but it made several overseas trips of some significance, two of which I went on with Jean Franchi to Rio via Dakar and Paris–Boston–Miami– Boston–Paris.

The two prototypes were coming to the end of their assigned tasks, once 002 had carried out a series of environmental flights from Prestwick and high-temperature performance tests in Madrid. Efforts to find natural ice using 002 failed and the work was transferred to 01 in due course. Following a demonstration flight for Princess Anne, 002 took part in the Weston-super-Mare Air Show but suffered a major failure on the left landing gear of the main retraction jack and the main side stay, which broke away when it was lowered in a 45° bank turn on returning to Fairford. John Cochrane took over control from Eddie McNamara and executed a successful landing with great skill, keeping the weight off the left landing gear by use of roll control. Fortunately, the left leg did not collapse and jacks were placed in position very rapidly and so what would have been a major accident was averted. 002 remained at Fairford awaiting disposal.

The time came to subject the intake control system to cold and ambient temperatures, which required operation away from base and Tangier was selected for trials by 01. The intake control laws were changed several times and surge margins were established both in level flight and during the course of various manoeuvers, i.e. pushovers and sideslips. The changes were made on the spot following analysis of test results with a portable computer, which BAC had installed in a second-hand furniture van for ease of transportation. John Cochrane was the spearhead of this part of the programme and did an outstanding job, although Bob McKinlay played a major role as well. After further intake tests a second trip to Tangier was necessary. The need to operate in the peripheral envelope had to be approached carefully as there always had to be a way out, but the duplicated system afforded the ability to operate two engines (one pair) using a law of wider surge margin. Nevertheless, this did not prevent an unfortunate incident when John Cochrane experienced all four engines surge in a pushover. After the flight he said to me, 'I thought that we had been sent for!'

Experience showed a wide variation in surge intensity depending on ambient temperature, mass flow, engine-power setting, and the number of engines affected. Consequently, the loads likely to be encountered were considered when planning each flight test. This was especially important on 01, which only had a safety factor of 1.3 as opposed to 1.5 on production aircraft. In-flight loads were monitored by the flight-test crew and limited to twelve surges per flight. Damage to the intake pressure sensor was a common occurrence to start with and some flights were curtailed due to this failure, but a 'fix' was found to eliminate this problem.

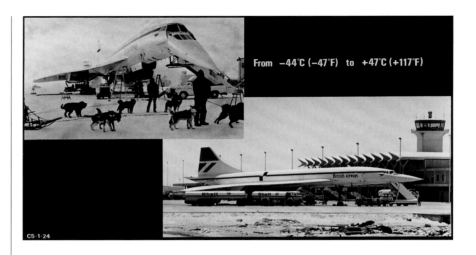

From −44°C (−47°F) to +47°C (+117°F)

02 during cold-soak tests at Anchorage (top) and 202 at Bahrain for high-temperature tests (bottom), 1974. (BAe Systems)

Casablanca replaced Tangier as first choice for testing because it afforded greater facilities and was further south. At one time engine surge tests seemed to be a way of life as production aircraft 1 and 2 were both subjected to finalising the basic laws, which had been set so well by 01.

We took full advantage of transiting to Anchorage with several important flights being made, which the sales department hailed as London–Paris. A flavour of the supersonic age was brought to the American Pacific coast by 02 which covered 27,000 miles in 27 flying hours: London–Mexico via Canada; Mexico–San Francisco; San Francisco–Anchorage; Anchorage–Los Angeles; Los Angeles–Lima; Lima–Paris via Caracas and Las Palmas.

Concorde was received with great enthusiasm and interest. At San Francisco, the Mayor, Mr Alioto, opened the press conference by saying: 'Britain and France have done a great job on smoke, noise and interference to the ozone. Noise levels are no greater than airplanes flying today and Concorde is coming to San Francisco to show what the manufacturers are doing to make the aircraft entirely acceptable. The city of San Francisco congratulates the manufactures and my personal prediction is that the US will certify Concorde.' Praise indeed, while the General Manager of Los Angeles Department of Airports, Mr Clifton Moore, said that he hoped the visit of 02: 'would accomplish some factual information on the effect of Concorde on the community. This Concorde is much improved over earlier versions and we have requested more operations into Los Angeles from the FAA to get more experience.' The Anglo-French airworthiness authorities permitted a small downward revision of the mandatory 1,000 hours of route proving as a result of this trip, coupled with those of the prototypes, 01 and production 1 and 2.

02 completed water-ingestion trials in a specially constructed water trough, which highlighted a problem of water spray from the main wheels entering the engine intakes. Although the engines kept running, a 30ft flame out of the exhaust showed that a remedy was needed. Bristol University came to the rescue and produced a solution in the form of a 'cow catcher' device to be fitted between the front wheels.

Clearing aircraft for natural ice has always been difficult because it is hard to find sufficient ice that will stick. 002 spent some time trying to find ice in Scotland, but did not succeed. Demonstration of protection against icing had become acceptable by flying behind a water spraying tanker. A KC-135 of the USAF was modified to do this and was in due course hired to position at Fairford where a number of flights were made. The great advantage of this method lay in the ability to fly in such a way that only half the aircraft was covered. The Ministry of Technology were not going to be outdone and produced a Canberra capable of spraying water. I became less enthusiastic when a frozen ice-ball of football proportions flashed past the cockpit window due to a fault on the spray valve. In spite of all this, the FAA still maintained an airworthiness requirement to fly in natural ice. The icing programme was transferred to 01 and a decision made to take the aircraft to the west coast of the USA where the required ice accretion was likely to be achievable. 01 flown by John Cochrane set a record on its way to Grant County Airport, Moses Lake, Washington, between Fairford and Bangor, Maine, of 2 hours 56 minutes. After some of the usual difficulties, which lasted two weeks, over 2 inches of ice was accreted, shed and re-accreted at 240k, 13,000ft. Handling, engine behaviour and systems operation were all satisfactory and the requirement was at last met. Tropical icing tests were also made at Nairobi. This ended the development programme on 01, which was then turned over for crew training of the British Airways nucleus group, who were destined to participate in the route-proving/endurance flying programmes.

FINAL PHASE AND CERTIFICATION

The introduction of aircraft 1 and 2 (201 and 202) started the final stage of development and of demonstrating compliance with TSS requirements leading to certification. 201 concentrated on all outstanding handling and completion of automatic flight-systems tests, including autoland. AICS checks for certification were also made. Flights by both CEV and CAA were one of the major tasks.

I flew 202 from Filton to Fairford on 13 February 1974 reaching M=1.43 during a quick squirt down the Bristol Channel. All forms of performance measurements covering take-offs, landings, climbs and

Concorde 002 flying behind the Canberra water tanker, 1973. (BAe Systems)

cruises were made on 202 and engineering tests at high ambient temperatures were carried out from Bahrain. The level of buffet after take-off seemed to be more pronounced than on 002, and so a trip to Toulouse for comparison with 201 was made within the first week. André Turcat and I flew both aircraft, which were not surprisingly any different from one another and concluded that the level of buffet was entirely acceptable even though it was slightly more than on the prototypes.

The certification work on the Air Intake Control System (AICS) required two trials at Casablanca dealing first of all with intake-ramp instability, instability of the outboard engines and marginal behaviour of the system during sideslips, and secondly proving that modifications had been successful. This being so, the system was deemed to meet all the airworthiness requirements over the whole speed range.

Much attention to the granting of a Special Category Certificate of Airworthiness was required for the start of route proving. At one time 201 and 202 were both at Casablanca when 202 turned up for a day to double-check satisfactory operation of the intake control system following a performance flight from Fairford of 3 hours 12 minutes, a flight of 2 hours 43 minutes from and back to Casablanca and then a return to Fairford lasting 2 hours 38 minutes, which was not a bad day's work for one crew.

In July 1974 the British Prime Minister Harold Wilson and the French President Valéry Giscard d'Estaing agreed an initial batch of sixteen Concordes. I received a telephone call from our Aviation Minister, Tony Benn, saying that he had heard of a pending trip to Bahrain scheduled for the following week and that he would like a flight and to bring some of the 'chaps' with him. When asked, the 'chaps' were the shop stewards from Filton, Weybridge and Hurn and we agreed on a party of forty. An enjoyable and relaxed day ended with a speech about the sixteen aircraft from the Minister and a vote of thanks for the flight for 'Tone' and Mr Trubshaw. Fame at last I thought.

The day before departure I had unwittingly dropped a propeller off BAC's Beagle 206S into Brookwood Cemetery. I flew 202 out to Bahrain for high-temperature performance and engineering tests routing over Russian air space to Teheran and on to Bahrain. Some shuttling to Kuwait and back to Bahrain took place as ground temperatures at Kuwait were higher than Bahrain, reaching 46°C. The test route from Bahrain was made eastward towards Pakistan from what was an ideal location without any form of restrictions. On the way back, a deceleration commenced abeam Dubai about 180nm from Bahrain. My wife, who was in Bahrain, said that she had heard us 'boom' which at the time I said was not possible as we were not fully aware of the 'secondary boom' made by Concorde. Later experience showed how right she was. Courtesy visits had to be paid to all neighbouring states in the Gulf area, necessitating trips to Kuwait, Doha, Dubai, Abu Dhabi and Muscat. This was fun and I enjoyed the time spent in the Persian Gulf very much indeed. Having completed the programme at Bahrain, we went on to Singapore in order to assess the response of a production aircraft to the runway undulations. Both Gilbert Defer of Aérospatiale and Gordon Corps agreed with my previous findings of unacceptability, which was only alleviated when the runway was relaid and a modified two-stage main oleo leg was introduced later on. Various abuse cases simulating engine failure and early/late rotation were included in the evaluation.

Dishevelled author in full flying kit after a test flight. (BAe Systems)

Simulator studies had evolved a special noise-abatement procedure for the preferential take-off runway of 31 Left at New York-Kennedy Airport, which involved executing a turn at 100 feet immediately after take-off. In-flight assessment included participation of D.P. Davies and Gordon Corps of the CAA and several captains of British Airways. Simulated engine failures and push overs were all made in order to show that there were no hidden dangers in the proposal, which came through all the assessments with flying colours. It was then a question of measuring the actual noise footprint, and so the Kennedy routing and measuring points were laid out in the desert around Casablanca, although the pattern at Casablanca required a right-hand turn instead of a left turn out of Kennedy for the Canarsie departure. After each take-off, climb- and cruise-performance tests were made. As some of the climb tests were made from low altitude, including zero rate of climb measurement at maximum take-off weight, the environment in the desert around Casablanca was ideal. Visits there were now so frequent that it became a second home. The precise and accurate handling qualities of Concorde were very well demonstrated by the ease of carrying out these manoeuvres even under failure conditions, and the noise-abatement procedure was approved.

On completion of the tests a VIP demonstration flight was arranged for which the Managing Director of BAC's Commercial Aircraft Division, John Ferguson-Smith, came out to Casablanca. His vociferous thanks to the first person who turned up to the pre-flight reception for attending turned out to be directed at the piano player, who had been hired for the evening, but this was only the start as it became known that a member of the PLO was one of the guests invited for the flight. The telephone wires to London were red hot before the night was out, but it was finally agreed to let the matter stand and that the individual would be shepherded by John Ferguson-Smith at all times. Unfortunately, No. 3 engine failed and surged during acceleration at M=1.7 as our escorted visitor was on his way to visit the flight deck. The flight was aborted and a return to Casablanca on three engines gave no problem, except that the disorder of their trousers required a protective sheet in order to preserve their dignity.

The noise results formed the basis of a series of meetings with the Port of New York and New Jersey Authority but it was two more years before permission was granted for operations by British Airways and Air France to begin. 202 made a further performance trial in Madrid, most of which was flown by the CAA or CEV for certification purposes. A special category Certificate of Airworthiness was granted by mid-1975 so that route flying could start. 201 and 202 were used for training Air France and British Airways for this next phase and the granting of a full C of A was almost complete.

The use of reheat and the variable nozzles produced one other problem which had to be addressed due to the inability to check correct functioning of the reheat system prior to take-off. The prototype practice of opening up the engines against the brakes was not possible on production aircraft engines due to the increased thrust of the Olympus 593-602 engines – on a wet runway, the aircraft would slide with locked wheels. Furthermore, the noise and potential jet-efflux effects made such a procedure unacceptable. Consequently, a procedure of preselecting reheat first prior to brake release followed by advancement of the throttles became and remains

Overleaf: Concorde 202 G-BBDG in flight, 1975. (BAe Systems)

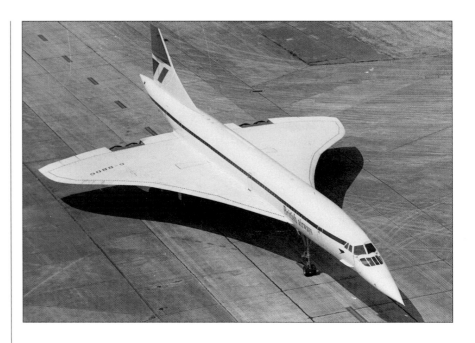

Concorde 204 G-BOAC, used for the route-proving and endurance programme. (BAe Systems)

standard practice. However, TSS Standard 6-0 required a single instrument to show a reading that correlates engine-thrust output during take-off and initial climb. There was therefore a need to link N1, N2, Pj, intake efficiency, nozzle efficiency and reheat status. Indication of movement of thrust reversers away from the forward-thrust position was also required for each engine. This indication had to cover the whole range of movement of the thrust reversing mechanism in the reverse positions.

In order to satisfy these requirements a row of three lights situated on top of the pilot's centre panel above the primary engine instruments is provided for each engine: Green – Clear to go; Amber – 'Con' light; Blue – Reverse light. A push button is provided to arm or inhibit the system. Automatic selection of engine contingency rating is derived from the arming button.

Concorde was awarded a full C of A in October 1975 by the French Authorities and in December 1975 by the British Civil Aviation Authority, although both 201 and 202 remained at Toulouse and Fairford respectively for further development after Concorde entered service. British Airways through the Flight Manager (Technical), Brian Calvert, formally objected to the granting of a C of A because a final solution to Concorde's tendency for overspeed above Mmo due to temperature shear (although finally defined) was not immediately available. I believe BA felt that greater urgency by Aérospatiale was needed. A solution had been demonstrated on 201 operating from Kuala Lumpur in October. I had joined Jean Franchi and Gilbert Defer for this series of flights which defined changes to the auto-pilot and auto-throttle systems which armed the auto-throttle systems in cruise so that they could intervene if M=2.0 was exceeded by reducing engine power. BA's objection was overruled but it scared the ARB Council into a declaration that a company test pilot had to be on board at the start of commercial service. This meant that either John Cochrane or I flew on every service at the start.

ROUTE PROVING

The two aircraft 203 (F-BTSC) and 204 (G-BOAC) that were allocated to conduct route-proving (endurance) flying were first used to tidy up outstanding C of A items when they flew in January and February 1975 respectively. Final air-conditioning clearance, auto-landing and cabin-noise final measurements were typical examples. Above all, checks on handling and engine behaviour throughout the speed range were made to ensure that what was now a genuine production aircraft met all the standards that had been set. Both CEV and CAA test pilots completed series checks to be doubly certain.

Final crew training of Air France and British Airways crews had to be completed before route proving could start, following the award of a special category C of A for each aircraft. 203 commenced on 28 May 1975 Paris–Dakar return and then Paris–Dakar–Rio de Janeiro via Dakar. Other destinations included Lisbon, Caracas, Shannon, Gander and Tangier. 204 started on 7 July 1975 to Bahrain.

The overall requirement of 1,000 hours route proving had been whittled down to 750 hours after the authorities were persuaded to give some recognition of what had gone on before, especially on 02. The airline crews had already had some exposure to Concorde at various times during the development programme. The BA Captains were Mickey Miles (Flight Manager), Brian Calvert (Deputy Flight Manager), Norman Todd (Training Manager) and instructors Pat Allen, Tony Meadows and Peter Duffy, with Chris Morley and John Eames following on to complete their flight training in Bahrain and Singapore after route proving had started. All the nucleus group as they were known had no trouble in converting to Concorde, although one change was made after the route proving was complete, following a discussion between Captain Norman Todd and me regarding the competency of all those involved.

Originally it was envisaged that there would be two phases in the flight trials. Phase one would be flown by a BA captain accompanied by a BAC test pilot. Phase two would be two BA captains. Within weeks of commencement, the CAA and the British Government changed their mind and required a BAC test pilot to be in command at all times, albeit from the jump seat. This went down very badly in BA and I received a telephone call from a very irate General Manager Flight Training, Captain Phil Brentnall, saying this was unlikely to be acceptable to BA. I was within an inch of having a row after such an arrogant approach but just managed to avoid one, explaining that the decision was not mine, so take it or leave it. That was the last I heard, although I did not like the arrangement myself as intervention from the jump seat was only possible in verbal terms. Cabin staff for 204 were provided by

Concorde 204 G-BOAC outside the hangar at Filton, 1975. (BAe Systems)

Concorde route-proving destinations. (BAe Systems)

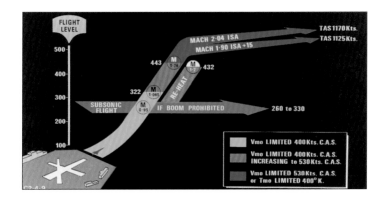

Flight profile of Concorde for climb and cruise assuming unrestricted climb clearance. (BAe Systems)

Concorde 204 G-BOAC at Bahrain during the route-proving and endurance programme, July 1975. (BAe Systems)

*Route-proving participants in Singapore, August 1975. The group includes Sir Geoffrey Tuttle, Vice-Chairman BAC Commercial Aircraft Division, and the author with his wife, Yvonne.
(BAe Systems)*

Singapore Airlines, Gulf Airlines and Air India because BA cabin staff were in dispute over Concorde rates of pay and arrangements. They fitted into the operation with great enthusiasm and ease.

I have never been completely convinced that route proving establishes anything as the real problems with a new aircraft always seem to occur after it is finally placed in the hands of the airline operator. Nevertheless, the Concorde operation gave confirmation of some weak points, notably the auto-pilot, as previously mentioned, and failures of the vaporisers in the Olympus 593 combustion chambers which surprisingly amounted to five on 204 and none on 203. One of these caused some embarrassment at Singapore after bringing the Australian Prime Minister Gough Whitlam from Melbourne, when an engine change had to be declared. He was most understanding, which is more than could be said for British minister Gerald Kaufman, who became decidedly ratty when he found that his flight was curtailed but I left him in the care of our Vice-Chairman, Sir Geoffrey Tuttle. Much of 204's programme was based at Bahrain followed by a period in Singapore, during which there was a week of supersonic flights between Singapore and Melbourne, flying across the middle of Australia at supersonic speeds. A look out of the windows showed that there was not much around to be bothered by a supersonic boom. The overland route ran just west of Alice Springs over desert-type country. Unfortunately, the use of a supersonic route over Australia never came to fruition when BA started service to Singapore because there were difficulties with Qantas on increased jumbo services from Sydney to

London in exchange for the supersonic route permission. Melbourne had to be the chosen destination because a long subsonic section of the route made a Sydney operation totally unrealistic in economic terms. The Australian government were very disappointed that their efforts to approve a supersonic route came to nothing.

Some complaints about booms were received from Malaysia as the aircraft proceeded down the Malacca Straits. Once again, I understand this was more to do with increased frequencies for Malaysian Airline Services (MAS) to London than any actual problem. A further period of operations from Heathrow–Gander were made by 204. Serviceability and despatch reliability were very good. 203 finished its share on 2 August 1975 having flown 367,900 statute miles in 125 flights, which totalled 375 hours 22 minutes block time (supersonic 258 hours 20 minutes) and carried 4,680 passengers. 204 completed on 13 September 1975 with 130 flights of 380 hours 43 minutes block time (supersonic 208 hours 33 minutes), covering 325,000 miles and carrying approximately 6,500 passengers.

One of the VIPs on a London–Gander–London flight was the Archbishop of Canterbury, Lord Coggan, who said to me as we cruised across the Atlantic at 60,000ft, 'I have never been closer to God'. 204 had

Sir Geoffrey Tuttle and the author being interviewed at Heathrow during route proving, August 1975. (BAe Systems)

Captain Tony Meadows in the left
seat with the author in Concorde
204, September 1975. (BA)

Concorde 204 taxi-ing out for take-
off at Singapore, August 1975.
(BAe Systems)

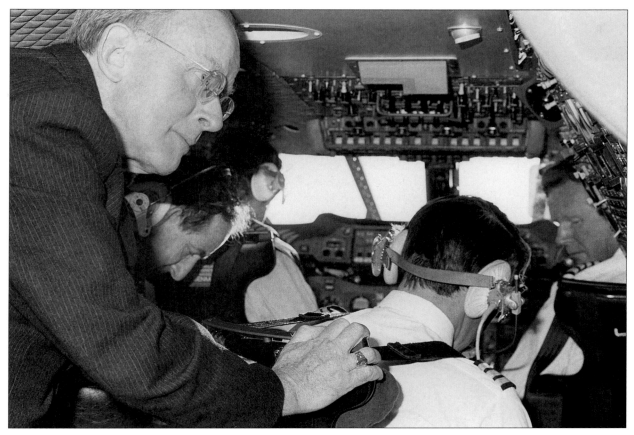

Lord Coggan, Archbishop of Canterbury, on the flightdeck of Concorde 204 during a flight to Gander, September 1975. Captain John Eames is in the right seat with the author on the jump seat. (BAe Systems)

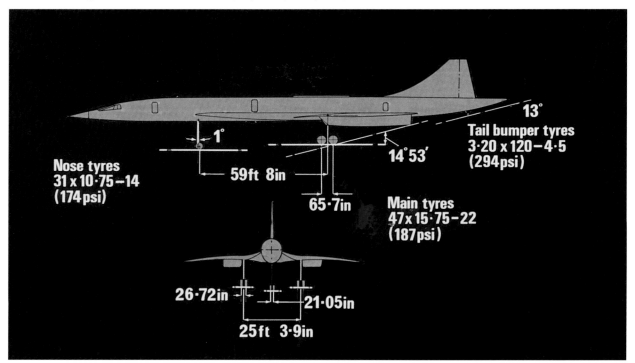

Tyre sizes used on Concorde with landing gear dimensions. (BAe Systems)

two incidents, one at Bahrain when a BA captain screwed the aircraft too tightly on the ground when parking so that damage occurred to the main right-hand landing gear oleo leg, which went flat over night and had to be changed. The other was during a night landing at Bombay, when on selection of reverse thrust, which lifts the nose requiring forward control column to counter it, the nose was allowed to lift a long way off the ground which scraped and holed the jet pipe on No. 3 engine. During the course of this, I was shouting from the jump seat in case the pilot allowed the nosewheel to drop back on its own as speed reduced. I found a willing volunteer in the Air India maintenance base on nightshift to put a patch over the offending hole. Bob McKinlay was horrified to see the patch when we arrived in Singapore 3 hours late, but it stood the M=2.0 flight from Bombay without any trouble. This type of event was the reason that I did not like sitting on the jump seat but still being in command.

On completion of the route flying both 203 and 204 went into their respective factories to be refurbished for airline service, although as a point of detail 203 was only loaned to Air France initially, and the stage was set for final certification. In the meantime, 02 flew to Canada for the opening of the new Mirabel Airport in Montreal returning to Paris in 3 hours 31 minutes on the twenty-fifth anniversary of the opening this route by an Air France Constellation in 13 hours 45 minutes. 201 continued to solve the auto-pilot problem at Kuala Lumpur, while 202 finished off a few miscellaneous tests such as a bird-impact windscreen assessment and the proving of BA's ground-running silencers at Heathrow. At the end of the route proving the re-organisation mentioned earlier took place within BA and Brian Calvert took over as Flight Manager (Technical).

The route-proving exercise once again highlighted auto-pilot deficiencies, not that the basic auto-pilot was at fault. The problem was caused by rapid changes of temperature when cruising at M=2.0 at high altitude when the tropopause is high. As the temperatures change rapidly, so does the Mach number. Consequently, if the auto-pilot is engaged in the 'Mach Hold' mode it will try to follow the Mach number in a violent manner. This caused high rates of climb and descent, finishing up in almost oscillatory conditions each time the temperature changed. Speed excursions between about M=1.8 and M=2.1 were experienced, the latter being well outside the approved flight envelope. Whereas it did not seem to worry the French too much, it was not acceptable to the CAA or BA.

It took some time for Aérospatiale, who were responsible for the auto-pilot, to come up with a solution which made use of the auto-throttle at the appropriate moment. Climb and cruise modes were created so that during climb Vmo is held until M=2.0/530k is reached. At that point the auto-pilot holds Vmo or M=2.0 or the maximum limiting temperature. The auto-throttle is armed during the climb. If the Mach number is increasing too readily, the auto-throttle engages automatically and pulls the engines back. I thought that this solution showed the ingenuity of the French designers at their best. Some people considered that the problem could have been anticipated. Although the conditions experienced were known about, the horizontal distance over which the temperature shear took place was a lot shorter than predicted and the statistics on frequency of occurrence were not sufficient to enable a true assessment of the consequences.

AT LONG LAST!

Commercial service started on 21 January 1976 with simultaneous take-offs from London to Bahrain and Paris to Rio de Janeiro. Take-off clearance was given at precisely the same moment to Captain Norman Todd, the captain of BA300 to Bahrain, and to Captain Pierre Chanoine, captain of AF085 to Rio. Few thought that the simultaneous departure would be met, but as is often the case with Concorde, they were wrong.

Both aircraft were at maximum passenger capacity and included HRH The Duke of Kent, Peter Shore, UK Secretary of State for Trade, Sir George Edwards and Alan Greenwood of BAC on G-BOAA; and Monsieur Marcel Cavelle, French Transport Minister, Pierre Giraudet, Chairman of Air France, Général Jacques Mitterrand, Chairman and Chief Executive Officer of Aérospatiale. Other passengers were from the USA, Germany, Italy, Sweden, Spain, Switzerland and Brazil.

The outcome of BA's objection to certification was solved in a political sense by appointing John Cochrane and myself as CAA Flight Inspectors, one of whom had to be present on every BA commercial service. A certain amount of backwards and forwards activity between BA and the BAC

The first commercial flight by BA to Bahrain with Captain Norman Todd (left seat), Captain Brian Calvert (right seat) and Senior Flight Engineer John Lidiard at the Flight Engineer's panel, 21 January 1976. (BA)

The team who flew the first commercial Concorde flight seen at Fairford, January 1976. Left to right: Senior Flight Engineer Lidiard, Captain Todd and Captain Calvert. (BAe Systems)

Concorde route patterns for Washington-Dulles. The position of danger areas required a special descent procedure. (BAe Systems)

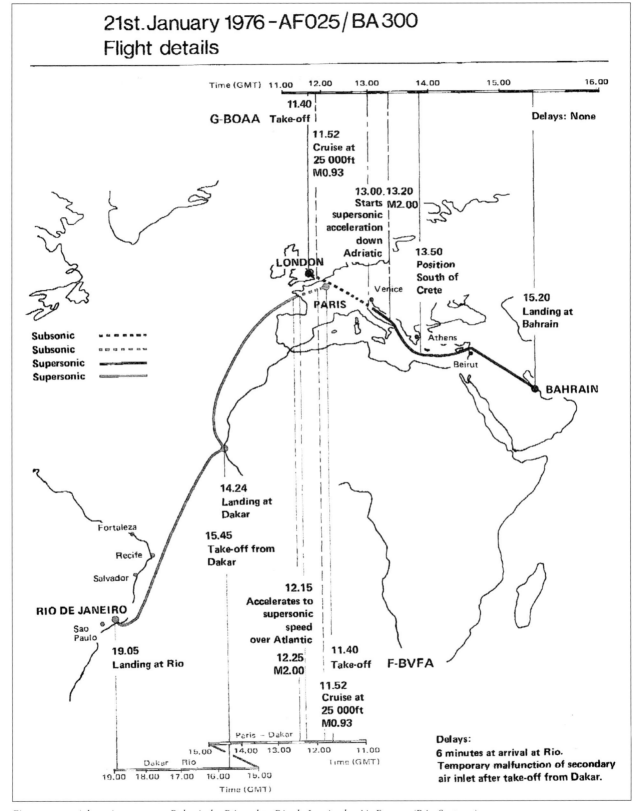

21st. January 1976 – AF025/BA 300
Flight details

Time (GMT) 11.00   12.00   13.00   14.00   15.00   16.00

11.40
G-BOAA Take-off

11.52
Cruise at
25 000ft
M0.93

13.00.13.20
Starts M2.00
supersonic
acceleration
down
Adriatic

13.50
Position
South of
Crete

Delays: None

15.20
Landing at
Bahrain

LONDON

Venice

PARIS

Athens

Beirut

BAHRAIN

Subsonic
Subsonic
Supersonic
Supersonic

14.24
Landing at
Dakar

15.45
Take-off from
Dakar

Fortaleza

Recife

Salvador

RIO DE JANEIRO

Sao
Paulo

19.05
Landing at Rio

12.15
Accelerates to
supersonic
speed
over Atlantic

12.25
M2.00

11.40
Take-off   **F-BVFA**

11.52
Cruise at
25 000ft
M0.93

Paris – Dakar

15.00   14.00   13.00   12.00   11.00

Dakar   Rio   Time (GMT)

19.00   18.00   17.00   16.00   15.00

Time (GMT)

Delays:
6 minutes at arrival at Rio.
Temporary malfunction of secondary
air inlet after take-off from Dakar.

First commercial service routes to Bahrain by BA and to Rio de Janeiro by Air France. (BAe Systems)

Company Secretary, Brian Cookson, took place in the process before we were both asked if we were prepared to do it. One cannot say that our presence was exactly welcome. It was a fatuous arrangement, anyway, as temperature shears that were the cause of the problem are not likely to occur between London and Bahrain. Personal egos were at stake and I had to creep on board with the rest of the passengers but turn left at the entrance into the aircraft and so to the cockpit. I was so incognito that I was missed off the invitation to the reception banquet given by the Amir of Bahrain at the Palace but some kind person, who I believe was Norman Todd, intervened at the eleventh hour and I attended. Sir Stanley Hooker relates in his book that: 'As I was about to thank the Minister of Foreign Trade for allowing us to come to Bahrain, he turned to me and said "What an honour you have done our country by bringing you magnificent Concorde here on its inaugural flight".' John Cochrane and I stood this farce for seven flights and then recommended to the CAA that BA should continue without us, which was accepted.

The inaugural flights went entirely according to plan and congratulatory messages passed between the Queen and the French President. On the 21 January 1976 the Queen wrote to Monsieur Valéry Giscard d'Estaing:

> On the occasion of today's inaugural flight by Concorde aircraft of Air France and British Airways, I send you and the French people my warmest congratulations. Today's flights mark the successful outcome of 14 years of close collaboration between our two nations. It is a source of pride that our countries have today inaugurated a new era in civil aviation.

Typical Concorde take-off. (BAe Systems)

It was indeed a historic day as supersonic civil passenger travel came to fruition after a very long countdown. BA had to manage with only one aircraft until mid-February when 204 (G-BOAC) was delivered following refurbishment.

On 4 February 1976, the combined and exhaustive efforts of the two governments, BA, Air France and the aircraft constructors to obtain landing rights into the USA for Concorde were rewarded by the US Secretary of Transportation, William T. Coleman, approving BA and Air France to operate two services each per day to New York and one service per day to Washington for a sixteen-month trial. However, the matter did not end there. Washington-Dulles was relatively easy because the airport is operated by the FAA which is linked to the Department of Transport. Some legal objections were easily overruled. This was not the case at New York, run by the Port of New York and New Jersey Authority (PNYA). The Coleman decision raised the sensitive issue of the rights of the federal government against the rights of states. The prospect of Concorde operations was too much for the noise-conscious 'locals'. Consequently, PNYA banned Concorde flights into and out of New York-Kennedy Airport, which was immediately challenged by the airlines who filed a suit questioning the Authority's right do this. PNYA responded with a requirement to conduct a six-month study of Concorde noise at Washington, London and Paris. Bearing in mind that actual results from trials at Casablanca had been in their hands for months, one did not have to be a rocket scientist to smell the political game that was being played. Other legal issues added further extension to the period which remained status quo until 1977 when Judge Milton Pollack of the Federal District Court ruled that the ban was illegal and should be lifted on the grounds that the delay in PNYA setting noise standards for Concorde was '. . . discriminatory, arbitrary and unreasonable'. PNYA appealed immediately to the Supreme Court, which upheld the decision of the Federal District Court and dismissed the appeal. Time had been slipping by while all this went on and so it was not until November 1977 that scheduled services to New York by BA and Air France commenced. However, operations to Washington-Dulles began on 24 May 1976 with departure times adjusted so that both aircraft landed at Dulles at the same time. In very quick succession and arriving on the ramp simultaneously, they raised their noses and visors in a synchronised salute. A special descent procedure was developed in order to comply with height restrictions, with certain danger areas and to meet the Mach=1.0 point. This procedure consisted of initial descent to 52,000ft followed by descent to 43,000ft at a constant M=1.3 with a preset altitude of 39,000ft at M=0.95.

A massive book was produced covering all known noise data and noise assessments, which showed that normal take-off flights from Runway 31 Left or 22 Right would be made at approximately 14 tonnes below maximum, producing a noise pattern similar to that of the Boeing 707-320 B, which met New York-Kennedy's noise criteria. Bob McKinlay and Henri Perrier gave a most detailed presentation covering all the facts. Concorde helped itself in some ways because of its exceptional ability to operate in crosswinds and tailwinds, its high level of performance and its ability to fly tighter patterns than most conventional large transports. The battle for New York was only won by real determination and dedication and those involved are to be congratulated and admired. Nevertheless, a heavy penalty was paid before this protracted affair was concluded and several airlines cancelled their options, influenced by the doubt of ever getting permission to operate into and out of Kennedy. I have always

Henri Perrier, originally Senior Flight Test Observer at Sud, succeeded André Turcat as Director of Flight Test. (BAe Systems)

Concorde 002 G-BSST at Yeovilton for the handover of the plane to the Fleet Air Arm Museum, 4 March 1976. The group includes Mr Gerald Kaufman MP, Vice-Admiral Sir Peter Austin, Sir Harold Wilson, Prime Minister, and Captain James Abraham. (BAe Systems)

wondered what would have happened if the American SST had survived. Later on, aircraft 201 made a short trial at Kennedy in order to validate the use of the two runways mentioned, which were known to be rough and undulating. Noise measurements were of course made and were all within limits. Enormous media coverage of the trial portrayed a grotesque scene, which many had to admit turned out to be a non-event.

One of the great supporters of supersonic transports was the late Bill Magruder, an ex-test pilot for Douglas and Lockheed who became Director of American SST development office, until the project was cancelled. He had flown Concorde at Fairford on two occasions and participated in the public hearings on Concorde in Washington DC. (BAC/Aérospatiale *Flight News* published Bill Magruder's testimony – see Appendix IX.)

There are various sad events, some human and some material, in the course of any long programme. 002 G-BSST was retired to the Fleet Air Arm Museum at Yeovilton to sit beside the BAC211 and HP115. Following the landing gear incident, the gear was locked down for its final flight to Yeovilton, where the runway length was not over generous, so that the landing weight had to be as low as possible and account had to be taken of high fuel consumption due to the locked down gear. Consequently, it was

FLYING SUMMARY	No./REGIST.	NUMBER OF FLIGHTS	SUPERSONIC FLIGHTS	BLOCK TIME hrs.:mins.	SUPERSONIC TIME hrs.:mins.	AIRLINE SERVICE	
						NUMBER OF FLIGHTS	FLYING HOURS hrs.:mins.
	001/F·WTSS	397	249	812:19	254:49		
	002/G·BSST	438	196	836:09	173:26		
	01/G·AXDN	269	168	633:10	217:03		
	02/F·WTSA	314	189	656:37	280:49		
	1/F·WTSB	423	247	909:52	339:25		
	2/G·BBDG	400	198	873:46	247:07		
	3/F·BTSC	173	160	505:08	316:54	123	178:44
	4/G·BOAC	188	164	558:04	269:35	46	137:30
	5/F·BVFA	11	10	37:13	16:20	154	346:19
	6/G·BOAA	17	14	58:15	22:39	98	247:22
	7/F·BVFB	8	8	30:32	12:34	51	144:19
	8/G·BOAB	2	2	8:36	2:51	—	—
TOTAL (May 31,1976)		2640	1605	5921:41	2153:32	472	1053:34

not possible to carry sufficient fuel to return to Fairford or Filton once committed at Yeovilton, so good weather was a necessity. Everything was in place for 4 March 1976 with the actual weather for Yeovilton given as clear, no cloud, good visibility. On arrival this was not the case, visibility was low and so was the cloud cover, necessitating a precision approach under radar. The Yeovilton controllers probably found the relatively high approach speed (150k in this case) disconcerting as 002 was not sufficiently well aligned with the runway for me to attempt a landing, so a second attempt had to be made which was successful, indeed as the fuel situation demanded that it should be. I was a bit put off by the Commander Air, Commander White, waving his bats as if it was a landing on to an aircraft carrier. I had hoped he would get out of the way and I feared that I might have killed him until his smiling face later appeared at the parking point. A reception committee including Prime Minister Harold Wilson, Gerald Kaufman, Vice-Admiral Sir Peter Austin and Captain James Abraham assembled for the official handover a few days later.

001 had already gone to Le Bourget while 01 remained at Fairford awaiting disposal having finished its programme during 1975. 02 made its last operational and delivery flight to Orly on 29 January 1976. It always

Concorde flying hours as at May 1976. (BAe Systems)

seemed a great pity that there was no further use for these aircraft, which had been the backbone of the development programme and flown such few hours.

These arrangements left 201 and 202 to finish off post C of A work and support the aircraft in service. 201 was primarily engaged in finalising the modified landing gear work, auto-pilot changes and clearing operations under Category IIIa conditions. 202 was almost immediately required for more performance testing when Rolls-Royce came up with a proposal for higher take-off thrust known as 'contingency' for use in emergency, by overspeeding the high-speed compressor speed (N2) by 2 per cent. This may sound straightforward but it necessitated a month's flight trial in Johannesburg and some ground running in Cape Town. The route Fairford–Robertsfield–Cape Town was made in a record 7½ hours, including the refuelling stop at Robertsfield, but could not be claimed because the use of Robertsfield in Monrovia had been given on the promise of no publicity as Apartheid was still in full cry and Monrovia is a black country. A day in Casablanca also had to be included in the 'contingency' clearance. Tests on a revised Air Intake Control Unit law and a week on static display at the SBAC show were included in 202's tasks.

The flight training simulator for Filton came on the scene early in the year and first of all had to be validated to the satisfaction of the CAA. It was a tight programme but approval was achieved in time for the contractual training class which started in March with flying training on 206 (G-BOAA) taking place in May. The simulator was financed and therefore owned by the Royal Bank of Scotland. This was, I recall, the first occasion when something to do with Concorde was not financed by the British Government. Walter Gibb, who had been chief test pilot before Godfrey Auty, spearheaded the initiative that produced this result, while Johnnie Walker covered the task of CAA validation. The first course, which included Captains Walpole, Myers, Bud, Butt, Benwell, Dyer and First Officers Orlebar and Lowe, was a disaster with a 33 per cent failure rate. BAC's training may not have been as good as it could have been but the real problem lay with the selection of the candidates. Several were below average on their existing fleets and just could not adjust to the quicker reactions required for Concorde. The ground-school portion was itself very arduous, lasting about six weeks. The methods required in the classrooms reflect the acquisition of knowledge required to pass the written technical examination of the CAA, which uses the multi-choice answer principle. The majority of training establishments have updated to more modern practical methods, which was well illustrated when some Braniff crews were trained at BAC while others were trained at Aeroformation, Toulouse. The apparent advantage of the multi-choice answer principle enables the examination paper to be marked by a clerk with no knowledge of the aircraft type. BAC were not permitted to fail any of the BA trainees on actual flying without their performance being witnessed by Captain Noman Todd. BA's own first course was not much better as far as failures were concerned but this continued until a more thorough selection process was introduced.

Both 201 and 202 remained assigned to providing the support for in-service aircraft which started an argument as to which aircraft should be retained in the long term. My view was that engine and intake problems were the most

Opposite: *Concorde flying past the air traffic control tower as it comes in to land at the Farnborough Air Show, 1986. (BA)*

likely areas to require attention but few others shared this view on the basis that systems of Aérospatiale responsibility such as auto-flight control, hydraulics, wheels and brakes normally produced the most problems. This favoured the retention of 201, although the aircraft needed an update to be able to accommodate 610 production engines. The future of Fairford clouded the issue even further and there was clearly a feeling among some BAC directors that the retention of 202 would lead to arguments to keep Fairford at a time when manpower reductions were required throughout the Commercial Aircraft Division (CAD). If Hurn had been capable of becoming the Flight Centre, a different view would have been taken and some level of support might have been coming my way. Hurn was not suitable in any shape or form at the time because the runway needed a considerable extension in length and the 'noise lobbyists' would have had a field day.

The hard fact was that Fairford was running out of work and the whole Flight Test Organisation and Facility could not be retained against a handful of production aircraft. A total of only sixteen aircraft, of which four were unsold, were to be built and of these only half were to be assembled in the UK. It was only the immediate advent of another development programme that could save Fairford. The unions were told all of this in November 1975 when representatives from all CAD sites met John Ferguson-Smith, the Managing Director, to be told that BAC had been informed by the Concorde Management Board on behalf of the British Government that they could not see the justification for keeping Fairford beyond mid-1976. However, the runway would be available as and when required for use by production aircraft from Filton during their two- or three-week production test programme.

The whole situation got completely out of step with reality when I formally announced that Fairford would close at the end of November 1976. The unions took the decision very badly, the Chairman designate of BAC (which was about to be nationalised) Lord Beswick, the Earl of Kimberley and many others became involved. Several cases for keeping Fairford were made to them, which all missed the vital point that there was not any work. A work to rule on aircraft 208 was almost immediate and a total 'blacking' followed. The dispute was eventually resolved with the assistance of the Engineering Employers' West of England Association but the delivery of 208 was delayed until the end of September instead of June. 210 flew in August and was delivered in December. 204 redundancies resulted as I was instructed to take a reduced flight-test staff and aircrew back to Filton along with 202, which in spite of all the forecasts kept flying until 24 December 1981.

Lord Beswick requested my presence to explain the whole saga. The intervention by this most approachable and friendly man made no difference. It was, however, quite a surprise to find the Earl of Kimberley also present at the meeting. For all my understanding, it was a sickening process breaking up a world-class team. It is with great envy that I have seen the Toulouse facility, which started on the back of the Concorde programme, transformed into the wonderful base for Airbus today that is second to none. This is the difference between a nation, irrespective of government, that intended to have a civil aircraft industry and one whose government's intentions have not been so obvious for many years.

A frontal view of Concorde. The two large vortex generators, classified as 'moustaches' by the French, are clearly visible on each side. The 'moustaches' were fitted to improve directional stability at high angles of attack. (Jonathan Falconer)

THE END OF
FLIGHT TRIALS

There was much more work to be completed after C of A than had been forecast and it was very fortunate that 201 and 202 had been retained for this. 201 dealt with problems of Aérospatiale responsibility such as Category III clearance. Proving the revised two-stage main oleo involved short visits to Gander, where the runway was sufficiently rough and undulating to produce the aircraft response levels that were needed. This modification was eventually fitted to all production aircraft.

From the end of 1977 all the flying on 202 was based at Filton, but this was a considerable anti-climax after the hustle and bustle of Fairford. Flights tended to be spasmodic and any significant task was greeted with a great deal of enthusiasm in spite of the fact that the Flight Test Organisation had been split into two buildings, Flight Operations (aircrew) and the Technical Block (Flight Test technical personnel), which were about ¾ of a mile apart. Nevertheless, we had to be thankful for small mercies and made it work. Fortunately, the major tasks that fell to 202 required operations from Casablanca for several weeks at a time. It was therefore with considerable envy that I witnessed Toulouse blossom towards what it is today. It is not surprising that a bid to conduct flight development and certify the Airbus A320 at Filton was laughed out of court by Bernard Ziegler and his team.

Minor performance improvement possibilities were identified by the Design Office by introducing extensions to the rudder and elevon trailing edge, changes to the rear ramp leading edges and further refinement of the intake laws. Handling, flutter and performance tests had to be made so that these changes and an increase in ramp weight could be offered as a package to the airlines, who indeed accepted them readily. These modifications were typical of post C of A development. Most of the performance measurements were completed during another stay in Casablanca, which was mainly directed to a modified Engine Control Unit and intake load measurements.

An enjoyable visit was made to open the new runway at Sharjah at the invitation of the Ruler, routing via Damascus because of the restricted weight out of Filton. The crew and Sir Geoffrey Tuttle, who accompanied us, all received a wonderful sword from the Ruler, who also gave everybody in the party a wrist watch.

If anyone imagined that engine surge tests were over, they were in for a surprise. A great deal of work was carried out on intake loads, stiffened

Overleaf: Concorde 202 G-BBDG was used extensively for all post Certificate of Airworthiness powerplant work and became a frequent visitor to Casablanca. (BAe Systems)

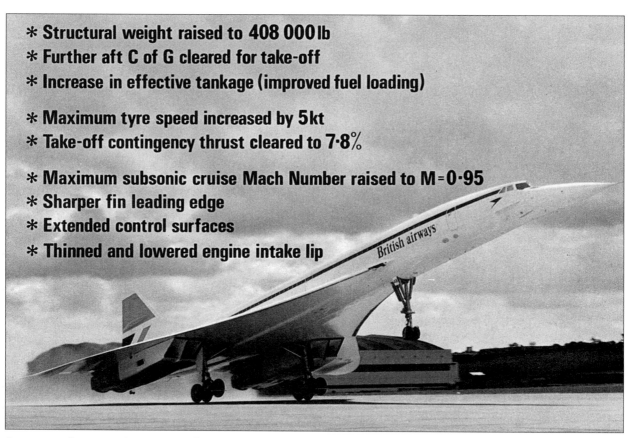

* **Structural weight raised to 408 000 lb**
* **Further aft C of G cleared for take-off**
* **Increase in effective tankage (improved fuel loading)**

* **Maximum tyre speed increased by 5kt**
* **Take-off contingency thrust cleared to 7·8%**

* **Maximum subsonic cruise Mach Number raised to M=0·95**
* **Sharper fin leading edge**
* **Extended control surfaces**
* **Thinned and lowered engine intake lip**

A summary of post entry into service performance improvements. (BAe Systems)

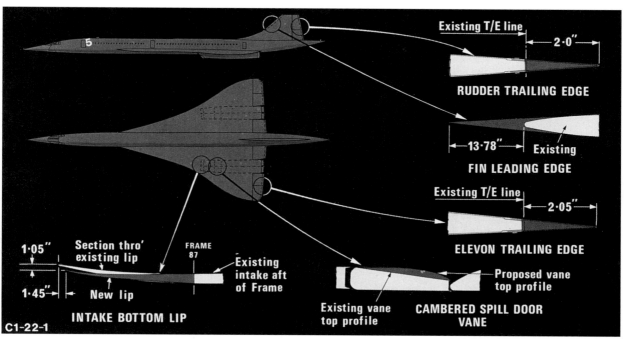

Details of air intake thinned lower lip and other aerodynamic changes. (BAe Systems)

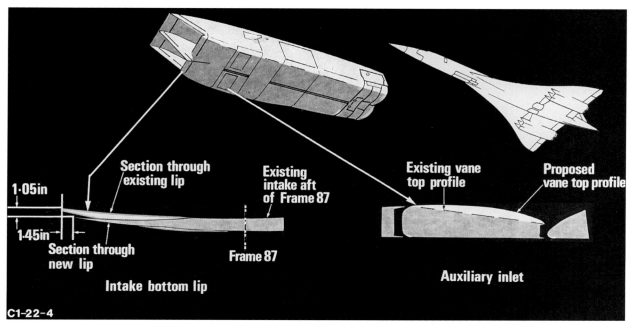

Structural changes of thinned lower lip, which gave a significant performance improvement. (BAe Systems)

Concorde 202 G-BBDG outside the special hangar built for it at Filton, 1985. This was the first time that 202 entered the hangar and it has remained there ever since. The group includes Captain David Leney, Captain Brian Walpole, Robert McKinlay, the author and Wensley Haydon-Baillie. (BAe Systems)

rear ramps and so on, all of which required deliberate surging. The majority of this was undertaken from Casablanca in order to get the low-temperature conditions which were the critical case. In August 1978, Rolls-Royce reported the possibility of surge due to over-fuelling the engine and this showed that the associated intake loads might be too high from a structural point of view. This was labelled as a high-pressure surge whereas previous surges that have been mentioned so many times were on the low-pressure portion of the engine. A special test box was fitted to one of the engines, which enabled the crew to inject a calculated amount of excess fuel into the engine which promptly and obligingly surged at the particular test condition of speed and altitude. As a temporary safety measure because of the projected high intake loads, the airline aircraft were restricted to 500k (normally 530k). The test programme was approached with some caution for obvious reasons. A full programme of engine surges up to M=2.15 were completed and the measured loads were significantly less than predicted, much to the relief of all concerned and therefore no modification was required. Nevertheless, the surges produced by over-fuelling were very hard and thoroughly unpleasant.

Concorde 201 F-WTSB specially painted by French university students at its retirement ceremony at Toulouse on the BAe twentieth anniversary of Concorde, 1979. (BAe Systems)

After entry into service the availability of an uprated engine showed that the intake was operating super-critically during cruise at ISA +5° with matched ramp angles of 7½ to 8°. In terms of efficiency, this was not good since the intake was operating at maximum capture. Wind-tunnel data showed that the installed performance could be improved by lowering the intake lip, which would allow ramp angle to be expanded, increasing the pressure recovery and demand for air. The overall benefit in terms of payload was assessed as 1,500 to 2,000lb. The lower intake lip was lowered 1.05 inches and thinned to 7½° but the sidewalls remained basically the same. It had also been determined that the cavity created by the auxiliary vane, which affects the flow in the intakes, is costly in terms of reduction in pressure recovery during cruise. Since the thickness of the trailing edge of the door could not be increased, it was decided to opt for a cambered shape which improves pressure recovery during cruise by about 0.2 per cent and by 0.4 per cent to 0.2 per cent during take-off. The modification offsets reduction in pressure recovery along the cowl side in the peripheral envelope and shock detachment at higher ramp angles. The

'White Tail' Concorde flies from Filton, 1978. (BAe Systems)

rear ramp leading edges are also rounded in order to eliminate high noise levels during cruise.

The flight test programme was arranged to demonstrate satisfactory operation of the revised intake configuration, which really amounted to full recertification, although past experience enabled specific critical points to be investigated. This had to be done before performance testing proper could commence. A new intake control law was established by ramp/spill door inching tests between M=2.0 and M=2.15. Surge margin checks on the ground operation as close to the surge line as possible (sea-level static conditions) were carried out along with checks at contingency rating to ensure that this had not changed. The majority of the programme took place from Casablanca in order to achieve temperatures as low as possible in the cruising altitude range of 50,000–60,000ft. The fitting of the thinned and lowered intake lips resulted in a general improvement in intake compatibility at high Mach numbers and a revised set of control laws was formulated to take advantage of the benefits. The package was sold to the airlines by the British Government, first of all to BA then Air France followed and it became the standard configuration. During the course of the tests 202 reached M=2.21. Use of the N1 wind down facility on 202 was necessary to reach this speed, so much so that there was no puff left to go any faster.

Most of 202's remaining tasks were engine and powerplant related and eventually came to an end on 24 December 1980. It was then parked outside at Filton and used as a 'Christmas tree' for spares to support the BA fleet. It became a real eyesore and would have deteriorated rapidly but BA decided to build a hangar for it at their expense, which is where it stands today. Various exercises have taken place over the years to assess the possibility of updating it for airline service, but the cost has always been prohibitive.

201 finished up with an enthralling ceremony at Toulouse when it was handed over to the Concorde Museum on the twentieth anniversary of Concorde. The aircraft had been painted in a cloak of many colours by French students and was kept in the dark, so that the gathering could not see more than an outline of Concorde until an array of special lighting was switched on to show this beautifully presented object. All this took place in a hangar at Toulouse attended by ministers, ambassadors, leading manufacturers' executives and a huge crowd of onlookers, of which 200 had been flown to Toulouse in Air France and BA Concordes chartered by Goodwood Travel. I flew to Toulouse and back in the BA Concorde with my wife and step-daughter. On the return flight, I asked one elderly lady if she had enjoyed the trip. She answered that she always enjoyed flying in Concorde and this was her thirty-fifth trip! Aérospatiale had laid on a great show but a much lower key affair occurred when 202 was pushed into its new hanger at Filton.

The price for new and advanced technology can be very high as shown by Concorde, when one reflects the extravagance of two prototypes, two preproduction and two production aircraft all going into retirement with very few flying hours: 001 – 812 hours, Le Bourget; 002 – 835 hours, Yeovilton; 01 – 634 hours, Duxford; 02 – 646 hours, Orly; 201 – 754 hours, Toulouse; and 202 – 803 hours, Filton.

Air France Concorde above the clouds. (Air France via Jonathan Falconer)

SALES PROSPECTS AND COSTS

There is little doubt that the original sales estimates for Concorde were optimistic and the potential of 240 Concordes by 1978 is clearly visible in some of the records and sales literature. The magic of 1978 was because this date was envisaged as the commencement of the American SST commercial operation. It was in this sense that Concorde was regarded as complementary to the American SST, monopolising the market until the American SST appeared, when it would be used on routes of lesser density. There is mention of 1,500 Concordes in service.

The sales prospects were encouraged by the fact that by 1967 there were 74 options on Concorde with the following airlines: British Overseas Airways Corporation 8; Air France 8; Air Canada 4; Air India 2; American Airlines 6; Braniff International 3; Continental Airlines 3; Eastern Airlines 6; Japan Air Lines 3; Lufthansa 3; Middle East Airlines 2; Pan American World Airways 8; Qantas Airways 4; Sabena 2; Trans World Airlines 6; and United Airlines 6. As can be seen from the list, practically every carrier was in on the act, which augured well for the future and gave great confidence to the British and French governments and of course to the manufacturers. Against such optimism, the future looked bright.

It was assumed at this stage that supersonic flight overland might be acceptable and it was realised that certain airlines, like Lufthansa for example, would need to fly supersonically over the UK. The acceptability of the sonic boom had been explored, first of all in the USA, then in France and the UK. Sir Archibald Russell and M. Pierre Satrè at the start of the Concorde programme suggested that at altitudes of 9 miles: 'the calculated over-pressure will in all normal conditions be less than that found to give rise to complaint. It may be that in unusual atmospheric conditions and with peculiar height of the tropopause, a noise resembling thunder will be heard. But this will not be an inevitable and regular occurrence.' However, a more pessimistic attitude was used later in evaluating sales potential, where it was assumed that supersonic flying would only be permitted over the sea and 'sparsely populated areas'.

The boom was of course well recognised before Concorde appeared, starting on the day that Chuck Yeager exceeded $M=1.0$ in the Bell X-1 over the Mojave Desert near Edwards Air Force Base. Most experiences of 'Le Bang Sonique', as the French called it, were associated with fighter-type aircraft. The Americans took advantage of the B58 supersonic $M=2.0$

Concorde model in the colours of Lufthansa. (BAe Systems)

bomber to gain further knowledge of the phenomenon. In 1961 Operation 'Bongo' took place over St Louis when B-58 bombers boomed by day and night. On 5 March 1962 a B-58 flew across the USA from Los Angeles to New York at M=2.0 in just over 2 hours. This was known as Operation 'Heatrise'. A second Operation 'Bongo' commenced on 3 February 1964 over Oklahoma with many buildings specially instrumented to measure the effects. This operation lasted for several months and amounted to some 1,250 booms. There were numerous claims for broken windows, but from Concorde experience on the west-coast route over Scotland, Wales and Cornwall, some of the claims at Oklahoma probably had nothing to do with Operation 'Bongo'. Britian was not going to be outdone and several trials over Aberporth, Bristol (without warning), Huntingdon and London using Lightning fighter aircraft were carried out without conclusion.

Najeeb Halaby of the FAA expressed great concern about the possible damage caused by sonic booms, whereas others were less concerned. The French were always more bullish about them than anyone else, in spite of a number of fatalities in a farmhouse when 'Le Bang Sonique' caused the ceiling to cave in.

In April 1967 Sir Giles Guthrie of BOAC stated that he did not believe that '. . . supersonic overflying would be restricted'. While Pat Burgess, Concorde Sales Manager, told a Press Conference that 'BAC had studied a mass of evidence on public reactions to US boom tests and feels that it will not be necessary to warrant a ban on overland flight'. Even Sir George Edwards, speaking to the National Aero Club of Washington about Concorde, is reported as saying that he believed that the sonic boom would in fact be '. . . acceptable over populated areas'.

The great opponent of SST, Bo Lundberg of Sweden, wrote a number of articles in the *Observer* condemning this. He was joined by Richard Wiggs, a schoolteacher who set up a citizen's group called 'Anti Concorde Project'. Six months later William Shurcliffe, a physicist at Harvard, started his 'Citizen's League Against The Sonic Boom', which was of great assistance to Senator William Proxmire who was determined to kill Concorde and the US SST. In reality the American SST was cancelled and Concorde production was terminated at the sixteenth aircraft, while the Tu144 never became a world runner. However, in 1969 Maynard L. Pennell, Vice-President of Boeing, said in an interview on returning from Moscow: 'The Tu144 is satisfactory for a prototype airplane' but 'is probably less sophisticated than Concorde today'. He mentioned 'small but important differences' in wing aerodynamics suggesting 'the Tu144 may not be as good as the Concorde in low speed and supersonic flight'. By US standards, 'Tu144 economics will probably be quite poor'.

Gradually, the airline option holders rejected Concorde, for a number of reasons in addition to the unforeseen rise in fuel prices and the uncertainty of obtaining landing rights at New York. The new technology of Concorde made it difficult for some airlines to assess its true commercial viability. The economic case for Concorde did not meet with universal approval. Both Pan Am and JAL (Japan Airlines) rejected the aircraft by their reluctance to move away from traditional accounting methods. A clear indication of the continuing development of improved models was essential and would undoubtedly have had a considerable impact on sales. Aircraft number seventeen would have been what is known as the 'B' model, incorporating some potent changes. The 'B' model would have enabled direct flights from Frankfurt to New York, for example. The wing was modified to include full span droop leading edges and extended wingtips. The powerplant was improved by increasing the mass flow by 25 per cent for take-off and about 35 per cent on approach by increasing the diameter of the LP compressor, replacing the single-stage LP turbine by a two-stage turbine and adding a bleed device to increase the surge margin of the LP compressor. Acoustic treatment of the intake and exhaust systems was also proposed. The aerodynamic changes improved the lift/drag ratio, resulting in increased range and noise performance for flyover and approach. The increased mass flow in the engine reduced jet-efflux speeds, thus the jet noise was substantially reduced as a result of the lower jet velocities. The hot part of the engine was retained and the

Concorde 'B' model with details of the radical changes that would have been made. These would have been incorporated on aircraft seventeen but production stopped at aircraft sixteen. (BAe Systems)

Concorde	Current (A610)	Developed	B622Y16L
Flying technique	Standard	Standard	New
Lateral	112·2 EPNdb	113·3 EPNdb	109·5 EPNdb
Flyover	119·5 „	110·8 „	111·3 „
Approach	116·5 „	112·0 „	107·5 „
Total	348·2 „	336·1 „	328·3 „

Droop leading edge

Section 'A-A'

Planform changes
New outer wing (E4)
Leading edge extended (BA10)
Droop leading edge introduced

yA551
yA503

Intake changes
Increased capture area
Thin lip (B 6')
Additional inlet vane
Revised main vane camber

Power Plant changes
Larger primary jet pipe & nozzle
Reduced reheat
Acoustic lining added
New L.P. compressor

turbine energy temperature remained unchanged. Reheat was deleted while an increase in thrust over the whole flight envelope, particularly in supersonic cruise, and an improvement in specific fuel consumption over the whole envelope, especially transonic, were achieved.

The airlines' concern over noise was directed more towards airport consideration and not the sonic boom. It was considered that fulfilment of these major ingredients could result in a world-wide requirement for 140 Concordes by 1980. It is easy to sit and be wise after the event over the forecasts. They were genuinely believed in at the time and they certainly had an impact on those engaged in the project to believe in it.

A number of small performance improvements were developed after entry into service and one of particular significance was in the form of a thinned lower lip of the intakes, which required a full in-flight programme of developing new intake control laws and certification. It was in fact full certification of the engine/intake all over again as already mentioned.

A great deal of effort went in to selling the five unsold aircraft following the departure of Pan Am. These were 214 and 216 on the British side and 203, 213 and 215 on the French. The possibility of a wet lease by Singapore Airlines reached the stage of firm proposals but the manufacturers could not commit themselves to the provision of all the flight crews for the four years required by Singapore Airlines. There were problems, also, regarding maintenance at Heathrow and provision of spares. A counter-proposal was made by BA which succeeded in reaching an agreement with Singapore Airlines for a joint service London–Bahrain–Singapore using BA aircraft, one of which G-BOAD had SIA colours painted along one side. This arrangement ceased in 1980 as the passenger loads were disappointing.

A combined effort to interest airlines in aircraft 203 produced a trip to Manila for Philippine Airlines and to Seoul for Korean Airlines. The first demonstration in Manila was a trip to Hong Kong for Madame Marcos to do some shopping. The trip only took 1 hour as there were no supersonic restrictions. The only problem was finding room on the aircraft for Madame Marcos's purchases. On return to Manila, one of the French sales team asked what the First Lady would like to do tomorrow. The reply was 'Go back to Hong-Kong!' So this was done. Korean Airlines were not very impressed by the economic presentation given by the British and French officials, but the visit afforded the opportunity to fly Seoul to London with technical stops at Singapore and Bahrain. This clearly demonstrated to me that this was too much for one crew and we were too tired on arrival at Heathrow. It was the equivalent of Hong Kong– London. Unfortunately, nothing materialised from this trip which originated at Paris-Charles de Gaulle Airport.

The 'white tails' eventually went to BA and Air France, so that both airlines finished up with seven aircraft each. The price paid was 'a nominal sum' in the words of official jargon, so much so that I upset a British official when I suggested that I might buy one myself.

During the period 1981–2, a major feasibility study was carried out in favour of converting a Concorde passenger aircraft into a freighter version for the American cargo airline Federal Express (FedEx). A number of design changes had to be embodied to accommodate the presence of freight in the fuselage as opposed to passengers. Systems such as oxygen,

Concorde fin showing the double rudder, in BA colours. (Jonathan Falconer)

air-conditioning, access to emergency lowering mechanisms for landing gear as the existing services would be covered by freight, all required attention. The original plan centred round the lease of three BA aircraft to FedEx. Subsequently, it became clear that the cargo carrier was seeking Air France involvement as well in order to secure French commitment to continuing support. FedEx requested a ten-year commitment from the British and French, although this was adjusted to seven years in the case of the latter. Neither the British nor the French governments acceded to more than five years maximum. FedEx start date would be September 1983 and the whole subject promoted enormous debate within the governments, manufacturers and the airlines concerned.

The FedEx operation was all part of the review taking place by Government ministers as to whether Concorde should continue. In the original plan of all three aircraft coming from BA, various assumptions of the probable fatigue life showed that the lease of aircraft 212, 214 and 216, which was the proposal, would result in the BA fleet being grounded before FedEx. This was of no consequence because the fatigue life assumptions were pessimistic, but in any case the whole affair never came to anything.

There can be little doubt that the view taken towards sales was optimistic and that the prospects of selling more that fifty to sixty Concordes were extremely remote. However, it is wrong to suggest that some of the option holders like Pan Am, TWA and Braniff were not serious contenders to purchase. Iran Air might have been another and I do not accept a statement I found in an old BAC sales document that said BAC only believed that fifty to sixty would be sold. If this is true, then some of our colleagues were not only very good actors but even bigger bull-shitters than I thought they were. The airlines did not like slippage in the programme, particularly the date for C of A, and it made a grave impression on several of the option holders. Airlines expect dates to be met, otherwise their whole planning operation cannot exist and they lost confidence in Concorde as a result.

As mentioned earlier, the problem of the sonic boom figured highly in sales deliberations because of its potential to limit routes, although there were a number of areas where supersonic flight overland was seen to be possible, such as Iran, Saudi Arabia and Australia. Some of this seems to have been forgotten as supersonic flights over Iran, Saudi Arabia and Australia were approved. Russia was of course another possibility.

Returning back to the sales aspect, one has to recognise the significance that the cost of the project had on the selling price and this is why sales and costs have been combined in this chapter. The cost estimate for the Concorde project started at £140 million but this did not last for long and it was the tendency for the all too regular increases to be identified that probably caused more anguish than the actual cost itself, because it was deemed to demonstrate administrative and technical incompetence. The first major increase occurred eighteen months after the start of work on the two versions – long and medium range – when at a special meeting of directors General Puget announced that he was recommending the cancellation of the medium-range version. No airlines had shown any interest in it and none of them believed that the sonic boom would be within the limits of human tolerance. Pan Am on the other hand was

Concorde's long, thin and highly distinctive fuselage. (Jonathan Falconer)

showing an interest with an option for six aircraft, but with a firm request to increase payload from 100 to 130 passengers. Cost estimates immediately increased to £280 million.

Soon after the increase had been identified, there was a change of government in the autumn of 1964 when a Labour administration headed by Harold Wilson was returned and which was immediately faced with a financial crisis. With a large trade deficit, the Prime Minister was being pressed by the Bank of England to reduce national expenditure drastically. A very strong opponent of Concorde was Richard Worcester, a well-known critic of British civil aviation policy, who had been advising members of the Labour Party that the American SST would inevitably deny Concorde any prospect of economic success, and that it was wrong to commit such a large part of the country's resources to such a project. A major financial loan of about £900 million from the USA was under negotiation. The previous Government had faced a number of visiting ministers and officials from Washington, who had repeatedly mentioned their regret in having to compete with supersonic airliners. A review of Government expenditure covering items of low economic priority, prestige projects and those of more

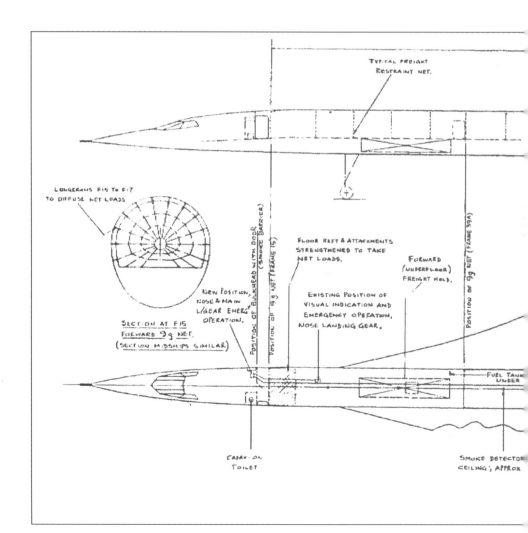

productive purpose was discussed at a Cabinet meeting. Concorde was axed without dissent but without regard for the Anglo-French Agreement, with its very important no-break clause, on a totally unilateral basis. It is important to realise that the long-range version that was to be axed bore little relation to that defined in the Treaty of Agreement (see Appendix I).

There was a no-break clause in the agreement on the grounds argued by Sir Julian Amery, Minister of Aviation, that it was not reasonable for either side to commit such substantial resources only for one partner to drop out in the middle of the programme. He suspected a French withdrawal. Both treasuries did not subscribe to this arrangement, but it stood and was important when following the change of British Government, Roy Jenkins was sent to France with clear instructions that the British Government wished to cancel the project on the grounds of cost. Harold Wilson had already been warned by his Attorney General that unilateral withdrawal could result in substantial damages being awarded by the International Court at The Hague and the doors to the European Common Market would be closed forever. President General de Gaulle had big plans for the glory of French civil aviation. Harold Wilson

Concorde modified for the Federal Express freighter version. (BAe Systems)

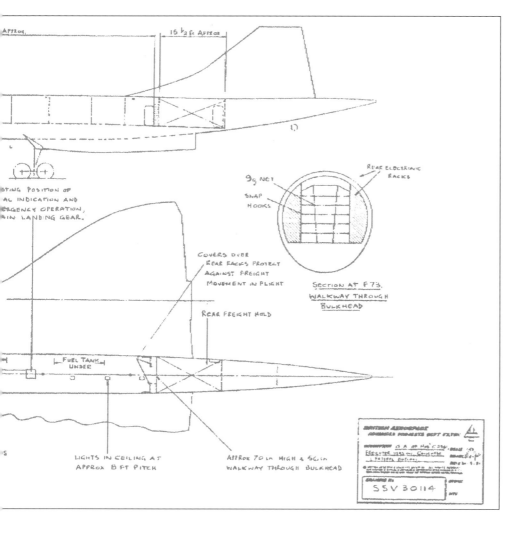

had to admit defeat, although only two months later General de Gaulle said 'Non!' to Britain's entry into Europe.

Cost and weight increases continued throughout the programme, and the cost increases included inflation. The British Government paid for everything in the development and no company money was involved until the later Conservative Government under Margaret Thatcher announced that it was not going to continue supporting and funding the in-service operation. It gave BA an option to buy all the Concordes, spares and spare engines, fund the in-service support themselves, and all other assets, or cancel their operation. Much to the surprise of the British Government officials involved, BA did not run away from the take it or leave it approach, although it did come pretty near to rejection. They negotiated a deal centred on £16.5 million for the five aircraft, which had been bought for £164 million out of Public Dividend Capital, plus spares, as well as the other two aircraft which were virtually given away at a consideration price of about £1 each.

In 1978–9 the £160 million was written-off in exchange for an 80/20 profit share arrangement which lasted until 1984, when BA bought all the assets for £16.5 million. In addition BA took over the treaty responsibilities to continue in perpetuity to supply support costs and spares which includes payments to British Aerospace and Rolls-Royce. This unique arrangement took some time to be fully absorbed and accepted by the French. All costs incurred by British Aerospace and Rolls-Royce are met by BA, which holds regular meetings with the other parties in order to monitor expenditure and authorise modification and other costs.

There is no doubt that the Concorde project suffered from not having a firm customer at the start. Earlier airline input would have saved money, as some of the original concepts on Concorde were flawed and did not reflect the way that airlines think. The particular areas that can be singled out for criticism include, for example, the moving map display. Who needed a moving map display for flying over the ocean and anyway the task of keeping it up to date when radio frequencies, for instance, change regularly, would have been enormous? The auto-monitor engine instrument was not liked, the airlines wanted existing equipment. The inertial navigation system made by Sagem-Ferranti was so sensitive during alignment that entry into the aircraft was actively discouraged; the airlines wanted Delco or Litton, which most of them already had. The engine starting by means of the gas-turbine starters on the prototypes or the MEPU on the first preproduction aircraft fell short of what the airlines required, which was a simple air start from a ground truck. Hydraulic gauges indicated 'Bars' because André Turcat said that this was the international definition of pressure. Maybe, but the airlines wanted what they had on other aircraft in 'lbs per sq ins'. The whole concept of the nose/visor arrangement on the prototypes was almost unbelievable. Apart from the almost total lack of forward vision when the visor was raised, the vibration at M=0.95 visor down (which was the subsonic configuration) was incredible and irrespective of expert opinion, the structure would never have lasted. The noise itself was horrendous. Failure to take account of the principles for the segregation of hydraulic pipes against the possibility of an engine-disc burst should have been got right first time, not the third. Future projects should not be afraid or ashamed to use proven equipment whenever possible. The inclination to start afresh on everything must be avoided.

BA AND CONCORDE

CHANGE OF ATTITUDE

Way back in the late 1960s and early 1970s no honest person would have thought that Concorde would not only be in service today but, certainly in the case of British Airways, be making a handsome profit. If BA had refused to take on Concorde in service support in 1983–4, Concorde would not be operating today. The British Government would have found a way with the French government to stop Air France's operation as well. This change of attitude by BA illustrates the fundamental change around that has occurred in the driving force. At the beginning, I always felt that the French were the dominant partner, whereas it was the British who held Concorde reviews with regular monotony: a 'review' was a polite expression of a desire to cancel. Although sales options dated back to 1963, it was 28 July 1972 before firm orders were received, five from British Airways and four from Air France.

Agreement was made on 28 July 1972 between BAC and BA for the sale and purchase of five Concorde Model 5102 aircraft at a basic contract price of £13,272,286 per aircraft, excluding spares, making a total of £66,361,430 at estimated 1974 prices. A similar contract was drawn up between Aérospatiale and Air France for four aircraft.

The lengthy agreement with BA covered all the normal aspects of an aircraft contract, including the French involvement, spares, after sales support, buyer's furnished equipment, training and delivery dates, delays, mock-ups, manufacturer's liability, reliability, etc. The delivery dates quoted were: 1st Aircraft – 31 March 1975; 2nd Aircraft – 31 May 1975; 3rd Aircraft – 30 June 1975; 4th Aircraft – 31 October 1975; and 5th Aircraft – 31 November 1975. These dates were subsequently renegotiated. By January 1976 the cost per aircraft had risen substantially.

Few were surprised by an order from Air France but the position of BA was different and there had always existed a body of opinion that was against Concorde. In 1965 Beverly Shenstone, Technical Director of BOAC (as BA then was, prior to its merger in April 1972 to form British Airways), whom I remembered from his days in BEA, classified Concorde as 'the largest, most expensive and most dubious project ever undertaken in the development of civil aircraft'. His doubts were based on the effects of the sonic boom and similar issues and furthermore he thought that the possibility of a profitable operation extremely remote. Because there was

such a lack of knowledge on supersonic transports, he favoured proving the concept by getting the RAF and French Air Force to operate it on an experimental basis. Shenstone was somewhat suspicious of the 'gang of optimists'. Fortunately, Morien Morgan, who was controller of aircraft at the Ministry of Aviation at the time, was an enthusiast, having set up the Supersonic Transport Aircraft Committee in the first place, although he was fully conscious of the fine balance regarding costs.

All through the early stages, the International Air Transport Association (IATA) was in the words of Sir George Edwards 'dead set against Concorde'. The Director-General of IATA banged on that the solution was to get rid of it. All this was coincident with a general airline depression and shortage of money, which meant that no one wanted to spend money on a new aircraft, especially one with so many unknowns. BOAC was bound by its Terms of Reference laid down in 1964 to act on normal commercial and financial principles. This led to lengthy discussions between BOAC and the Department of Trade and Industry (DTI) because BOAC regarded it as a bar to purchasing any Concordes. This was regarded as out of date at ministerial level and BOAC as a nationalised carrier was expected to order Concorde in the national interest. No

Concorde number fourteen, originally one of the 'White Tails'. (BA)

Concorde in Air France colours at Paris-Charles de Gaulle with two Boeing 747s in the background, 1991. (Jonathan Falconer)

directive that they had to make purchases was issued, but no doubt there were a few nods and winks behind the scenes. Sir Keith Glanville was Chairman of BOAC when the order was placed on completion of further financial deliberations between the DTI and BOAC.

By 1974 David Nicholson was Chairman of BA (1971–5) and expressed the wish of the BA Board to the new Secretary of State for Trade, Peter Shore, that Concorde succeed. However, he was still looking for financial protection in such a high-risk scenario. Sir Frank McFadzean (1976–9) was decidedly anti-Concorde for economic reasons. The BA Concorde Project Director had the task of introducing Concorde into BA revenue service. He did not have great enthusiasm at the start because as he said recently 'the results being forecast with great precision and fairly high degree of optimism – were appalling'. But as he said himself, he had the job of putting Concorde into service and he had to change his spots. His other big problem was where could BA operate? Bahrain was the only option for the time being. In Air France the counterpart of Gordon Davidson (BA Concorde Project Director) was Jean-Claude Martin with whom he struck a good informal relationship. Air France did have the advantage of routing to South America.

The pendulum continued to swing and another hurdle had to be assessed in 1979 when a new Conservative Government took office. It wished Concorde to continue if this could be done within the bounds of price control. At the same time a new attitude towards nationalised industries began to emerge. Sir John King (Lord King of Wartnaby) took over as Chairman of BA from Sir Ross Stainton in 1981 with a clear brief to prepare BA for privatisation. Recent results showed a need for cutting costs and increasing revenue but Lord King was keen to retain Concorde. Staff morale needed an uplift and this was regarded as being an important element to achieving profitability.

In May 1982 the Concorde Division was set up on the principle of a profit centre under the Concorde Flight Manager (Technical) Captain Brian Walpole who was appointed General Manager of the Concorde Division. This proved to be the turning point in the survival of Concorde thanks to the wisdom of Lord King and his Chief Executive Roy Watts. Brian Walpole introduced Jock Lowe, a Senior First Officer on Concorde, who later rose to Captain and then

Lord King of Wartnaby, Chairman of BA in 1981, without whose drive, leadership and wisdom Concorde would not have succeeded. (BA)

Director of Flight Operations, before his present appointment as Commercial Manager, Concorde. Jock Lowe is the longest serving Concorde pilot. The appointment of two practising pilots broke previous tradition. Lord King gave Brian Walpole two years to turn Concorde into profit. While Brian Walpole considered every possible way of increasing revenue, Jock Lowe concentrated on cost reductions. With full support from above they transformed the Concorde into a story of commercial success by making the operation profitable. With all due respect to their predecessors, the new approach was far more dynamic, far seeing and ingenious. When Colin Marshall (later Lord Marshall) arrived as Chief Executive in 1983, he immediately retained the focussed Concorde team. The Concorde Division really ran as an airline within an airline. Captain David Leney succeeded Captain Brian Walpole as Flight Manager (Technical) Concorde and was another great contributor to the success of Concorde.

Lord Marshall, current Chairman of BA, who supported the retention of Concorde when he joined the airline as Chief Executive in 1983. (BA)

The profitable operation resulted from reducing costs by reducing crews, discounting and increasing fares – it was in fact a cost-based operation. Charters were introduced at this time, starting modestly but in the year 2000 have become 5 per cent to 10 per cent of the whole operation. Some of the first charters originated from members or ex-members of the Concorde Division. Others came from people like Mrs Jackie Bassett from Bath who ran a Concorde Fan Association Club.

In 1980 the Select Committee for Trade and Industry, chaired by Sir Donald Karberry, became involved in calculating the costs to the British Government of supporting Concorde in service. The Committee was ordered to investigate costs when their examination of Government departments' expenditure indicated that some £30m of tax-payers' money was to be spent on technical support for Concorde in 1980–1. In the course of its enquiries, it was revealed that in the period 1980–1 to 1984–5 net Government expenditure might reach £123m. The Committee was critical of some of the DTI's assumptions and of the profit estimates of BA. However, the Committee emphasised its admiration of the technical achievement and acknowledged the 'spin-off' in high technology. Furthermore, there was no desire on its part to compromise safety.

A high proportion of the support costs came from the Major Fatigue Test Specimen at Farnborough. Therefore, the matter of the continuation

Lord Tebbit with the author and Captain Brian Walpole at the House of Commons, c. 1976. (BAe Systems)

of Concorde services by BA and Air France (with or without FedEx) or cessation on an agreed basis, became the subject of numerous meeting between Government officials, manufacturers and the airlines, and was interwoven with the fatigue life resulting from the level of testing. Briefs for ministers in both countries followed a strict timetable.

The real interest of the Select Committee lay in the question 'who pays?'. Consequently, the overall wish of the airlines on whether or not to continue was of paramount importance. The matter of reducing costs was already in place without the intervention of the Select Committee.

In 1982, I had taken over the duties of Concorde Project Director at BAe in addition to my other duties within the company and so was closely involved in the next crisis, which occurred in August and within only a few months of Brian Walpole's appointment. The Under Secretary of State for Trade, Iain Sproat, wrote to Lord King informing him that the Government intended to cease funding the support costs of Concorde and did BA wish to take over the responsibility of paying primarily BAe and Rolls-Royce. BA was under no illusions that refusal on its part would mean termination of Concorde both here and in France. The scene in France had changed when François Mitterrand became president in 1980 in that he was prepared to review Concorde's financial position. The subject was on the agenda for a summit meeting in 1981.

But here we had a situation where Concorde started by one Conservative Government was about to have its legs pulled from under it by another Conservative administration twenty-one years later. BA responded that it was prepared to examine the case but it would take some time to come up with the answer. It was given a year for this activity before the axe would finally fall. It was a major task for BA because there were many matters to be examined, especially the manufacturer's estimates for future in-service support costs. Both BAe and Rolls-Royce agreed to consider jointly the level of support required with a view to achieving reductions where possible. By the autumn of 1982 BA, BAe and Rolls-Royce had identified a list of considerable potential savings and Lord King then wrote to Iain Sproat, Parliamentary Under Secretary of State for Trade, stating that BA had concluded, following its major review, that it could take over the future costs of supporting Concorde in-service, subject to agreement being reached on certain points. Norman Lamont (later Lord Lamont) Minister of State for Trade and Industry, informed Parliament that the points raised by BA would be discussed by all the interested parties.

BA's response was regarded as being very constructive and this resulted in the Government deciding to extend funding support beyond 31 March 1983, so that there was adequate time to complete the discussions and for BA to raise new contracts with the British manufacturers. However, it was

Presentation of FAA airworthiness certificate to Mick Wilde and the author. (BAe Systems)

made clear that the funds earmarked for supporting Concorde in 1984–5 had been switched to other aerospace projects, which meant that there was no funding available beyond 31 March 1984. In order to achieve this date, contracts between BA and BAe and Rolls-Royce had to be in place by 31 December 1983, so that the new arrangements could take effect from 1 April 1984. BAe and Rolls-Royce in the meantime were given formal notice that their support funding contracts would terminate with effect from 31 March 1984. This was indeed a tight scale to be met. A review team was set up under the joint chairmanship of Bruce McTavish, by now Head of Concorde Branch at the Department of Trade and Industry, and of the Planning Director British Airways. It involved DTI, Department of Transport, Procurement Executive the Ministry of Defence, and representatives from all departments concerned in British Airways.

There were a number of concerns on all sides, including the French, who had been kept informed by Norman Lamont via his opposite number M. Fiterman, Minister of Transport. The main concern referred to a scenario where BA decided to stop operations but Air France did not. Both BAe and Rolls-Royce were especially concerned as to what was expected of them in such an eventuality, and what protection would be provided against any claims from the French for breach of contract, which could come from Aérospatiale, SNECMA, Air France or the French government. This is not the place to further the enormous detail that followed between all the parties. BA consistently wished to continue providing suitable financial and legal arrangements could be made, including a programme of fatigue testing to achieve adequate life. This needless to say required even more meetings before an arrangement acceptable to all concerned was reached. Although the proposal nearly floundered, in the end BA agreed to take over all UK support costs, which came mainly from BAe and Rolls-Royce from spring 1984 under the arrangement whereby all assets covering airframes, engines and spares were taken over by BA. BA's final acceptance of the proposal came as a surprise to some of the officials who had thought that BA would pull out.

During the course of this lengthy escapade, BAe represented by Mick Wilde, John Dickens and myself together with representatives of Rolls-Royce and BA appeared before the Select Committee in 1982. Officials from the DTI briefed us not to include any financial information in our written submissions as these would be correlated by the department and, anyway, the proceedings would be very straightforward. Sir Donald Karberry congratulated Mick Wilde on a beautifully written and presented document and then roasted him alive on the basis that despite being part of a financial enquiry, 'reference to the £ was nowhere to be found'. This brought the meetings to its toes.

As already stated, the BA operation of Concorde had to start very modestly, London to Bahrain because it was the only destination available in January 1976. Approval to operate to Washington DC came in May 1976. New York was always the goal but this did not occur until 1977 by which time Washington loads were declining in spite of extending the route to Miami. An interchange agreement with Braniff, which covered Washington to Dallas subsonic and which was flown by Braniff crews came to an untimely end when Braniff went bust. Although Washington–Dallas was flown subsonic there was clearly a desire by Braniff to increase the operation to South America. Braniff had a particularly buoyant South American network and had an identical arrangement with Air France.

Concorde required FAA certification which involved some relatively minor changes to the hydraulic system following failure of one system (in fact this change was an improvement to the basic aircraft) and slight alterations to the windscreen wipers. Different registration numbers were also needed so that the Braniff section could operate with an N registration whereas the British equivalent was G and French F. For example G-BOAA became GN9411 and G was covered over in Washington en route Dallas and re-appeared Washington–London.

Another deal thought to be a promising arrangement with Singapore Airlines was negotiated by Gordon Davidson and resulted in a London–Bahrain–Singapore service with one side of the aircraft G-BOAD painted in Singapore colours and BA colours on the other. This started in December 1977 but was suspended after three flights due to problems of flying supersonic down the Malacca Straits and was reinstated in January 1979. Thanks to politics, this route ran into major difficulties on supersonic routing and gave an inadequate financial return. There was little demand, averaging about forty passengers, whereas seventy to eighty were required. The advent of the Boeing 747-200, which could fly London–Singapore non-stop, had a major impact.

London–New York started at seven flights per week (one daily), then ten and now holds at fourteen (two per day). The Washington route came to an end in early 1994 simply because everyone wanted New York and not Washington. The late 1980s saw the first service to Barbados commence as a charter, then becoming a scheduled service, although mainly in the winter. In 1998 there were forty flights to Barbados. In 1999 the service operated between November and April with a very high demand. New York, of course, remains the mainstay of the profit, although the other significant contributor is the charter business, which

Concorde G-BOAD with Singapore Airline colours on the left side and British Airways on the right when it operated under an agreement between BA and Singapore Airlines in December 1977. (BAe Systems via Jonathan Falconer)

Passengers and crew on Concorde having arrived at Filton from London, 9 April 1999. This flight was to commemorate the first flight of 002. (BAe Systems)

BA Concorde flying the Royal Standard, February 1984. (D. Leney)

Captain David Leney (centre) with his crew prior to a royal flight with HM The Queen, February 1984. (BA)

Passengers sit in pairs in Concorde's narrow passenger cabin. (BA)

CONCORDE: THE INSIDE STORY

Captain Mike Bannister, current Flight Manager (Technical and Training) Concorde, who continues the line of outstanding BA Flight Managers on Concorde. (BA)

has expanded considerably since it began in 1982–3 and which, as already stated, equates to 5 to 10 per cent of the whole operation – that is about 200 sectors per annum. The advantages of charters are that they permit access for everyone, that they provide better publicity than scheduled services and they make a profit. It is now big business in the hands of organisations like Goodwood Travel and Superlative Travel, both of whom have an extensive destination network ranging from Christmas in Lapland, Moscow and the Bolshoi Ballet and Christmas Shopping in New York. I had the experience of chartering a Concorde for Wensley Haydon-Baillie, to whom I was aviation advisor between retirement from BAe in 1986 to 1998 when he ran into financial difficulties. The requirement was for a flight around Scotland calling on various relations plus a supersonic dash to M=2.0 on the way down the North Sea and back to London-Heathrow. The passengers were all invited guests of Haydon-Baillie. I was somewhat intrigued when I asked what the price would be and the reply came 'What are you in for?' The thought had not crossed my mind. One could not charge someone who was already paying my fees.

In 1999 Goodwood Travel chartered a Concorde from BA to commemorate the first flight of 002 with a plan to fly London–Filton, then Filton–Fairford to simulate the actual first flight and then a supersonic flight over the Bay of Biscay back to London. Unfortunately, the war in Kosovo was on and Fairford was full of USAF bombers and tankers, so making a landing there was prohibited. A substitute flight round the south of England was performed before the supersonic return to London. I was on board as a guest of Goodwood Travel and had a tremendous, if nostalgic, day with the ninety-nine passengers, one of whom had got the seat allocated for my wife at the last minute as she was unable to come due to illness. The flight was commanded by Captain Mike Bannister, Flight Manager (Technical) Concorde, and Captain Jock Lowe came as well, sharing the commentary with me.

Air France have operated for some time using five Concordes and their operations have followed a similar pattern to British Airways, now serving Paris–New York only and operating charter flights. The Paris–Washington route extended to Mexico City in 1978 lasted until 1981, while the service to Rio and Caracas ended on 31 March 1982. The Air France operation has always been boosted by French presidents who have used Concorde when attending international summits. Air France's charter activity has improved considerably with time and in 1992 Concorde Spirit Tours chartered an Air France Concorde for circumnavigation of the earth – a distance of 25,137 statute miles – and achieved a record of 32 hours 49 minutes 3 seconds. Several British travel agents, including Goodwood Travel, charter Air France Concordes in addition to those operated by British Airways.

Her Majesty the Queen and His Royal Highness Prince Philip used Concorde for the first time on 2 November 1982 and again in February 1984 for the start of a three-week tour of the Middle East, beginning at Kuwait and calling at Bahrain and Riyadh. A further trip to Barbados was made in March 1989.

British prime ministers have marked important meetings by using Concorde. Jim Callaghan (Lord Callaghan) flew to Washington in March 1977 followed by Margaret Thatcher (Lady Thatcher) in 1986 en-route to Vancouver to visit Expo 86. In 1995, John Major used Concorde to fly to a meeting with President Clinton in Washington, while Tony Blair has been to Washington and Denver on Concorde.

The British Ryder Cup team travel by chartered Concorde and even Pepsi-Cola came in on the act on 2 April 1982 when an Air France Concorde was painted blue to advertise Pepsi-Cola's new can. Richard Noble, one-time holder of the world landspeed record, set another record on 22 November 1987 to make the tenth anniversary of Concorde operations into New York-Kennedy Airport when he made the crossing three times in one day. Even now new routes, new ideas and new ventures are being continuously considered.

I still see a great deal of BA as a member of the Flight Operations Safety Board, chaired by Captain Mike Jeffery, Director of Flight Operations. The sheer professionalism and dedication to flight safety of this board comprising all the senior management captains, with representatives from engineering and from the British Airline Pilots Association, fills me with much admiration and pride. In these days when it seems that no opportunity to 'knock' BA is missed by its opponents and in the media, I wish that more people could see what goes on behind the scenes to ensure flight safety. I myself have always had a great desire to live.

Those who have operated Concorde are relatively few and a close relationship has been running for some years through the Concorde Dining Society which holds an annual dinner at the RAF Club each year. It was founded by David Ross, a Concorde captain for many years, who very sadly died in 1999 soon after retirement. In fact his last flight was taking Concorde off from the Farnborough Air Show and returning to Heathrow in 1998. I saw him off on this flight. A principal guest is always invited and there is usually an attendance of seventy to eighty people.

The reliability of Concorde is very important, because substitution of a subsonic alternative in the event of delay is not what the customer has paid for. Consequently, a standby Concorde is supposed to be available at Heathrow every morning after a directive from Lord Marshall to this effect.

For most of its life in BA, a dedicated Concorde team has existed because the maintenance task is not an easy one. Safety plays a major part of the engineering team's activity and a safety board similar to the Flight Operations Safety Board was created a long time ago. The Concordes 'lived'

Captain Mike Jeffery, Director of Flight Operations BA, another distinguished professional. (BA)

Some members of the 'original' team, left to right, back row: Peter Barker, Captain Norman Todd, Captain Peter Duffy; middle row: Captain Tony Meadows, Captain Keith Myers, Captain Pat Allen; front row: Captain David Leney, author, John Cochrane, Captain Brian Calvert and Captain Brian Walpole. (Author)

Concorde G-BOAA in the hangar, Technical Block B at the BA Maintenance Base, London-Heathrow. (BA)

The author in front of Concorde at Filton on the thirtieth anniversary of 002's first flight. (BAe Systems)

in Tech Block B hangar until about two years ago when the lease of that building expired and maintenance operations were transferred to Tech Block A, which is the current arrangement. There is a great deal of Concorde 'know-how' among the team that keeps Concorde flying, and includes some people who worked for me at Fairford during the development programme.

Each year some new record or activity of interest involving Concorde has occurred on a regular basis. In February 1985 a London–Sydney charter flight was achieved in 17 hours 3 minutes, followed almost immediately by London–Cape Town in 8 hours 8 minutes. In February 1996, Captain Leslie Scott covered New York to London in a record-breaking 2 hours 52 minutes 59 seconds, which is detailed below by Captain M. Bannister:

One of British Airways' fleet of seven Concorde aircraft set a new transatlantic record last night (7th February 1996) when it was flown from New York's John F. Kennedy airport to London's Heathrow in just 2 hours 52 minutes and 59 seconds. The sleek Anglo-French airliner averaged over 1,250 miles per hour throughout the crossing – about 22 miles every minute. She broke her own fastest transatlantic time by over 1 minute.

The Supersonic jet, under the command of Captain Les Scott, left the British Airways Terminal New York 4 minutes ahead of its 1.45 p.m. local schedule, 6.45 p.m. London time, was airborne at 1.51 local and

A wheel change in progress in the hands of a most dedicated team. (BA)

touched down on runway 09R at Heathrow at 9.44 p.m. – over 40 minutes ahead of schedule.

Whilst Captain Scott, who has been flying Concorde since mid-1994, piloted the aircraft his Senior First Officer Tim Orchard and his Senior Engineer Office Rick Eades liaised with Air Traffic Control Authorities on both sides of the Atlantic to make the record crossing possible.

The record breaking aircraft, G-BOAD, first flew on 25 August 1976 but has completed under 6,000 flights and less than 19,000 hours. She flew round the world in 1995 on 23-day Concorde Air Cruise visiting the United States, Pacific islands, Australasia, Beijing, India and Africa.

During the flight the passengers were treated to the usual superb Concorde service. The Cabin Service Director, Derek Bowles said that 'The passengers and whole crew were very proud to be part of another exciting milestone for Concorde'.

In welcoming the outstanding team effort Captain Mike Bannister, Flight Manager Concorde, said 'This records shows that our beautiful, sprightly and youthful aircraft can still set new standards in Customer Service over 20 years since she first flew in British Airways colours. The aircraft are in great shape and will be ahead of the pack well into the next Century.'

THE FUTURE

Time changes many things and the future of supersonic transports is one of them. A few years ago the future looked pretty bright and in 1991 BAe was working closely with Aérospatiale on the concept. An international study group consisting of BAe, Aérospatiale, Boeing, Deutsche, Airbus, Douglas with Alenia, Mitsubishi, Kawasaki and Fugi, with Tupolev following slightly later, was formed to examine the market, environmental and certification matters and business compatibility. These studies went very well. BAe and Aérospatiale were able to draw heavily on Concorde experience and in order to avoid losing 'know-how', Robert McKinlay (who did so much on the Concorde programme) when he was Chairman of British Aerospace Airbus, appointed a retired BAe design engineer, the late Jim Wallin, who was Chief Power Plant Engineer on Concorde, to archive Concorde experience from interviews with other individuals engaged in the programme and from the many reports and documents that were available. Sadly, old age and poor health have taken a heavy toll on the 'originators' of Concorde.

Throughout the same years, Boeing had over 100 engineers working on a future SST under funding from NASA. At that time there was a general feeling that the future AST would be dominated by Boeing, which was not going to be left behind second-time around. Boeing's dominance has changed considerably against the greatly improved performance and achievements of Airbus, which is now a very strong competitor for the No. 1 slot. Recent reports indicate that NASA funding has dried up, although it is possible that work on finding a suitable propulsion system continues. At the Andrew Humphrey Memorial lecture at the Royal Aeronautical Society in 1998, Sir Ralph Robbins, Chairman of Rolls-Royce and an engineer of considerable standing, cast considerable doubt on the future of ASTs due to the number of aircraft that will be required to do the task and suggested that the number was unlikely to exceed 100. This number when set against the projected development cost does not make economic sense. This is at considerable variance with figures produced by some manufacturers, where figures of nearly 1,000 are recorded. All the excitement of the early 1990s when one felt that the next generation SST was about to pop out of the door has gone a bit quiet. At one time a project launch of mid-1998, production 2000, first flight by 2003, certification and entry into service at the end of 2005 were all set as potential targets.

The thought of a genuinely world-wide project would pose organisational problems of such propensity that the late Alistair

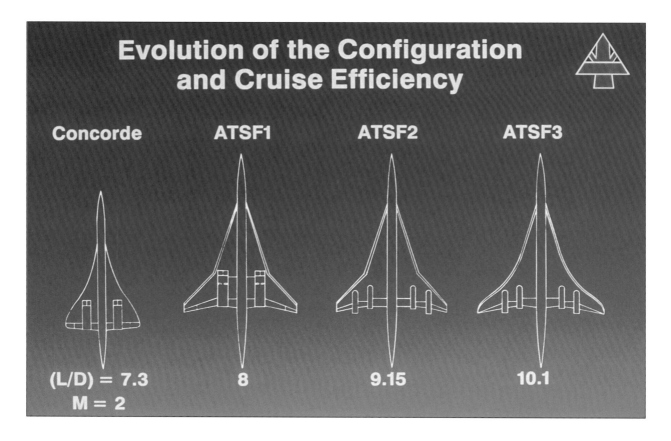

Evolution of the Configuration and Cruise Efficiency

Concorde	ATSF1	ATSF2	ATSF3
(L/D) = 7.3 M = 2	8	9.15	10.1

Future developments compared to Concorde. The significant improvement in lift/drag ratio is illustrated. (BAe Systems)

Cumming of British Airways just laughed at the idea. The studies that have been carried out on an American, a European and a world-wide basis, have identified the basic specification of carrying 250–300 passengers over a minimum range of 5,500 miles at speeds between M=2.05 and M=2.4.

In its early investigations BAe Airbus took Concorde and applied the technology of the time in order to produce a datum aircraft, which should not be confused with an actual proposal. Such a move illustrates the progress that has to be made in the years that have followed in order to produce a successful second generation supersonic transport.

The USA has been in favour of M=2.4 on the grounds that such a speed is relevant to utilisation on long routes so that two trips in a day can be made. However, this situation is not so simple and actual scheduling has to be evaluated in detail to uphold such a case. AST operations will be between main airport hubs and therefore actual departure and arrival times from and to the spokes play a major part in determining the whole operation, including fleet mix.

Europe, on the other hand, believes that M=2.05 is satisfactory and that the small benefits of the higher speed bring two main disadvantages. First, higher operating temperatures will have a direct impact on structural material choice and on secondary materials such as cable insulation, tank sealant, oil and grease, which will lead to higher overall cost due to the extra research required, whereas the Concorde experience on this is mammoth. Secondly, the air-intake configuration of Concorde has an external compression system which is inherently stable and thanks to Concorde is a proven background. The higher speed will not permit the use of an external compression system and a mixed compression system will be required in order to limit external drag. A very fast reacting control system to stabilise the shock system will be needed because instability in the shock system can lead to an 'unstart', which from the Lockheed SR71 experience can be violent and impossible to recover without shutting down the engine.

Significant technology requirements have been identified by the Working Party on Second Generation Supersonic Transport formed by that splendid organisation the Royal Aeronautical Society. The working party is chaired by Robert McKinlay and Captain Jock Lowe is another major contributor, so there is no shortage of Concorde expertise. Some of the requirements can be summarised as:

- 35 per cent higher supersonic life/drag ratio than Concorde. This is 10 per cent higher than that achievable at today's technology
- 20 per cent higher subsonic L/D than Concorde
- 40 per cent lower structural weight than Concorde
- 10 per cent lower supersonic cruise specific fuel consumption than Concorde
- 20 per cent lower subsonic cruise specific fuel consumption than Concorde

A Boeing project of Advanced Supersonic Transport. (BAe Systems)

- Approach and terminal manoeuvre speeds no worse than Concorde
- Dimensionally capable of using airports for subsonic aircraft. The AST envisaged with 3-class seating for 300 passengers is about 320ft long
- Operational reliability at subsonic aircraft level
- Demonstrably capable of meeting noise and emission standards at time of project launch and offer to airline operations. This is probably the most difficult task because agreement on noise emissions has to be on a genuinely international basis. The use of these issues as a political football must be avoided. Some feel that this points the project in the direction of international collaboration as being essential
- The landing characteristics will require special attention and certainly some form of flight control surfaces at each end of this 'long cigar' are likely to be needed
- Range growth must be demonstrable
- Various engine options need further examination and the development of a variable cycle engine may be necessary. A low drag nacelle no more than 7–9 per cent of total aircraft drag will also need to be developed. Reduced jet velocity is also required
- The AST will be 50 per cent bigger than Concorde and twice as heavy because of the increase in passengers and increased range

These are great challenges but I believe that they can be met. The big question is when? The immediate answer is not known, but when one considers that there have been almost 100 years of manned powered flight so far, of which thirty have provided supersonic passenger flying, it is difficult to believe that it will never happen. There is ample evidence that people are prepared to pay for a 3-hour journey: Concorde to Barbados, starting as two flights per year and now up to forty is a prime example of the demand. Therefore it is reasonable to assume that a 20 per cent surcharge is likely to be acceptable. This in turn means that design and production costs will have to equate to such a formula and this will have a major impact on the timing of the project, which will need to sell about 500 aircraft. This is of course at variance with the view expressed by Sir Ralph Robbins, Chairman of Rolls-Royce. Adding it all up, means simply that a M=2.0+, 5,500-mile supersonic commercial transport is some way off.

The airline requirement can be summarised as:

- Capable of operating at fare premium which will increase airline profitability overall
- Clearly capable of meeting noise and emission standards at time of airline commitment
- At least 5,000nm range at entry into service with significant development potential
- Supersonic cruise at least M=2.0
- three-class layout
- Capable of efficient mixed subsonic/supersonic operations
- Capable of using today's airports
- No unusual operating or crew training requirement

The question of an executive supersonic aircraft is under full investigation, especially in France, but the question is will companies be able to afford one? No doubt their shareholders will hold strong views. BAe produced a project for a twelve-passenger supersonic executive aircraft as long ago as 1986. Perhaps such an aircraft could operate within an airline for the benefit of businessmen and women. Air transport has had no history of going backwards, so the scene may change unexpectedly and rapidly. A technical solution to the sonic boom would of course alter the whole situation but is not in sight at present.

Proposals to date have dispensed with the droop/nose arrangement on Concorde in order to save weight. As the aircraft undoubtedly will be fitted with leading edge devices, the high nose-up attitude of Concorde on the approach will be less and the view overall will be supplemented by artificial vision. This may be fine for missiles and military purposes but not everyone believes that it has a place on a civil aircraft. God gave men two eyes, why not use them? Full stability augmentation will be included on any AST, which will enable tailored control laws to dominate handling qualities in the same way as has already happened on subsonic aircraft that are heavily augmented.

The British Aircraft Corporation carried out many studies in the late 1960s and early 1970s on the performance benefit accruing from the inclusion of a second control surface on Concorde, but the gains in this case were not sufficient to justify the cost and complications. Some argue that a foreplane degrades airflow over the wing, thus reducing lift. Also, that it can be destabilising as it moves the aerodynamic centre forward and that it worsens pitch-up at high angles of attack. No doubt solutions can be found to any of these potential problems. Obviously the matter of fitting a tailplane comes into the reckoning, but any tailplane that produces the right level of pitching moment is likely to be unattractive from a weight and cruise drag point of view.

However, all this goes to show the tremendous advantage that Concorde's background in design, manufacture and airline service provides to those who will be engaged in producing the second-generation supersonic transport. In recognising the technology that is available for any new venture, one must not lose sight of the Russian contribution. NASA has had recent experience of using a modified Tu144 for some experiments connected with future ASTs. The Tu144 began life in 1971 and was regarded as a formidable commercial competitor by the FAA. Its appearance was welcomed by SST proponents in the USA, France and Britain, although Britain's attitude towards the Tu144 was rather negative in terms of its rivalry. Neil Armstrong, the first man on the moon, described the Tu144 as 'a fine looking aircraft – as good as the best kind of products we're putting out'.

The story of the Tu144 is covered extensively in a book called *Soviet SST* by Howard Moon, a historian who lives in Virginia, USA. Providing the Russians disclose everything, the amount of information available must be enormous. The Tu144 failed to materialise as a commercial proposition and was not helped by two crashes, the second of which at the Paris Air Show on 3 June 1973 has not been satisfactorily explained and the cause is a matter of conjecture in my view. One explanation was that a

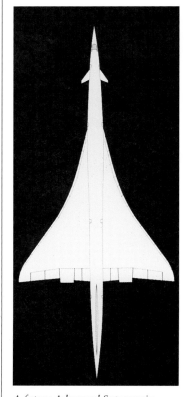

A future Advanced Supersonic Transport. (BAe Systems)

153

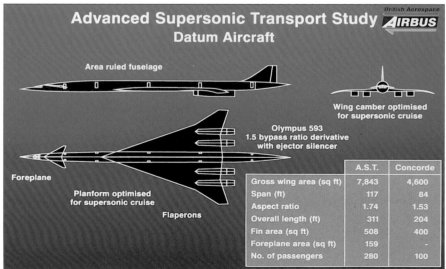

Details of an Advanced Supersonic Transport compared with Concorde. (BAe Systems)

	A.S.T.	Concorde
Gross wing area (sq ft)	7,843	4,600
Span (ft)	117	84
Aspect ratio	1.74	1.53
Overall length (ft)	311	204
Fin area (sq ft)	508	400
Foreplane area (sq ft)	159	-
No. of passengers	280	100

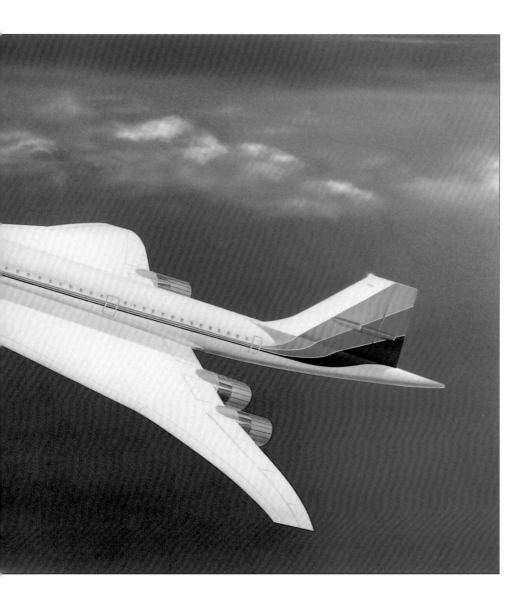

A possible Advanced Supersonic
Transport configuration. Note the
increased size and addition of fore-
plane compared to Concorde.
(BAe Systems)

camera being held by one of the crew was dropped into the control
column cone in the floor, jamming the controls when pilot Mikhail Kozlov
made a violent evasive manoeuvre in order to avoid a Mirage III which
had appeared unexpectedly in his path. Other onlookers talked of a 'stall'
induced by fuel starvation as a result of the very steep climb following its
final pass. Whatever the cause, the aircraft finished up in an almost
vertical dive at low altitude. Kozlov almost managed to recover but in so
doing the aircraft must have been overstressed as the right wing broke off,
followed by the left wing and then full disintegration. The presence of the
Mirage III and the fact that Kozlov's display time was curtailed by the
managers of the air show after he had arrived in Paris, when he had
rehearsed a longer timed display in Russia, were cited as factors in laying
the blame at the door of the French authorities. It is much more likely that
the prestige contest between Concorde and the Tu144 played a major role
in the catastrophe.

Concorde used as a supersonic engine-test vehicle. (BAe Systems)

It is the disappointment in the lack of openness on the cause of the crash that leaves a lingering doubt on the reliability of any information on the project as a whole. The most remarkable aspect of the Tu144 programme was the speed of configuration change from the very rudimentary prototype to the more elegant production model, which incorporated a new engine intake layout and a more sophisticated wing plus the addition of canards. Some Western visitors to the manufacturing facility were seemingly impressed by some of the production techniques. Any future AST will not be short of technical background when one considers the difference in knowledge when Concorde was conceived compared to the present day.

Concorde could be used as a supersonic test vehicle providing: sustained supersonic testing of powerplants up to M=2.2 (proven) or M=2.3 (with development); early fixed configuration models with existing engines; to final AST standard for performance and noise validation. Full-scale testing of aerodynamic features: leading edge flaps; arrow wings; trailing edge flaps with foreplane or tailplane.

Japan has been engaged in supersonic and hypersonic programmes and will no doubt be a leading contender to participate in any international venture. The final outcome of all the work mentioned will have been scrutinised over and over again. Even issues like the secondary boom, with people now talking of tertiary boom as well, will have been aired to death. Someone needs to grab the reins and say 'I want some!' and get on with it!

THE DEATH OF A DREAM

BUT THE PHOENIX RISES AGAIN

By the summer of 2000 Concorde had flown to 250 different destinations around the globe. Wherever the visit occurred, this supersonic masterpiece attracted thousands of supporters just wanting to catch a glimpse of the aircraft as it arrived or departed. For example, an estimated three-quarters of a million people turned out to see Concorde when it arrived for its first visit to Toronto.

The dream, which began in the minds of a few visionaries in the fifties, became the dream of millions of people. For some, that dream of flying at twice the speed of sound has already become reality but for many, many more it remains a goal, a burning ambition to experience the thrill of sitting on the edge of space for themselves.

Brian Trubshaw's opening words in this book are that 'it is not unreasonable to look upon Concorde as a miracle'. On 25 July 2000 at 16.44hrs local time, just west of Paris-Charles de Gaulle Airport, the dream assumed the shroud of a nightmare and the miracle was shattered along with Concorde's immaculate 32-year safety record. Concorde F-BTSC of Air France crashed into a hotel in the Paris suburb of Gonesse, killing all 109 people on board and four on the ground. The unimaginable had happened.

This is a chapter that Brian would never have wanted to write but reluctantly agreed to do so once the Air Accident Investigators had established the facts. However, he was also positively steadfast in his decision not to write anything until Concorde had her airworthiness certificate reinstated. Sadly, he never had the opportunity to express his opinions regarding the crash that involved the aircraft he was so passionately enthusiastic about, because he died on 24 March 2001.

Jock Lowe, formerly Commercial Director of the British Airways Concorde Fleet, presents below the crash investigators' findings together with his own conclusions.

For the family and friends of those who perished in this tragic accident, and those who raced to the scene in the sadly futile attempt to rescue survivors, the dream can never be restored. As with all aircraft accidents, work began immediately to establish the chain of events and the issues behind them that had caused the unthinkable, with the clear intention of preventing them from happening again.

But this work to make Concorde, and perhaps all commercial aviation,

The image that seared itself into the memories of millions: Air France Concorde F-BTSC in its final death throes, 25 July 2000. (Associated Press)

safer and more efficient did not just start after the Paris crash. From the time Concorde was handed over to British Airways and Air France during late 1975, experts of many disciplines within the industry examined and implemented ideas to continually improve the world's most tested aircraft. The list of improvements would need a separate publication to do them justice, but some of the more important concepts include changes to systems, aerodynamics, crew and maintenance procedures.

One of the first changes to Concorde made shortly after its introduction to commercial service was to the centre of gravity procedures on take-off. The original limit of 53.5 per cent mean chord position placed a limit on fuel loads. In consultation with the manufacturers and in particular with John Cochrane, Brian's deputy through the test programme, the available centre of gravity limit was changed to 54 per cent chord position. The significant benefit of this was the increase in maximum fuel load by 1.5 tonnes, and this in turn increased the number of additional possible diversion airfields.

There were a number of conditions which needed to be fulfilled before this revised process could be used and not least the clear, unequivocal instruction that 54 per cent chord position was 'the limit' – no further rearward shifts of centre of gravity could be tolerated. John Cochrane, who completed most of the extremely precise and difficult flight envelope exploration in this area, made everyone aware of the dangers associated with further aft movements at slow speeds. Later changes to fuel loading techniques (the 'High Level Increment') increased the maximum fuel payload by a further 1.5 tonnes, improving range and diversion capability.

Wheels and tyres have been areas for much attention. This followed a tyre burst incident to an Air France aircraft at Washington in June 1979 and further less significant events experienced by British Airways and Air France in subsequent years. As a result of the studies and risk calculations a series of modifications were introduced. Some of the more important

airworthiness changes were the installation of a tyre deflation mechanism using strain gauges on the undercarriage. Activation of a warning from the system below 134 knots calls for the flight crew to reject the take-off. Increased protection to the normal hydraulic braking system and inspection of wheels and brakes before every departure, and reinforced wheels and tyres to increase their load bearing and damage tolerance capability.

These modifications reduced but did not eliminate the frequency of tyre and wheel incidents. Furthermore, in 1981 British Airways stopped using re-treaded tyres and later Air France followed suit. Despite these changes, in 1992 a British Airways aircraft suffered a loss of tread and damage to a water deflector which is located in the front of each main undercarriage. A fuel tank was hit and a small puncture appeared. An optional modification adopted by British Airways to add steel reinforcing to the water deflector resulted.

The air intakes on all supersonic aircraft are crucial to their performance and safety. Small changes to the aerodynamics on the intakes were applied and various modifications to software and hardware improved the reliability over a very short period of time. It was found that the fibreglass tubing that carried most of the electrical wiring over the engine installation had begun to chafe, resulting in damage to the wiring looms. All intakes were removed and rewired using new materials.

However, new materials were not the answer with the engine turbine blades. Continued and detailed analysis of engine component changes gave a different answer. It was realised that the end portions of the titanium

Grounded: British Airways' fleet of seven Concordes awaits news of its fate at the company's engineering base at Heathrow. (British Airways/Adrian Meredith Photography)

A large section of Kevlar fuel tank lining held by Jim O'Sullivan, BA's Director of Engineering, who was responsible for the entire re-certification programme. Looking on is Captain Mike Bannister, Flight Manager Technical of BA's Concorde fleet. (British Airways)

billets from which the blades were produced contained microscopic bubbles. By discarding these portions the reliability of the blades and engines improved greatly. Many other engine reliability modifications were also incorporated to increase the time between changes.

The Concorde, which uses hydraulic components for flying controls, air intakes, nose and visor, undercarriage, brakes and some fuel pumps, works at pressures which are 33 per cent higher than common on other commercial aircraft. The original hydraulic seals were shown to be less adequate than required at these pressures and working temperatures, so a new composition of sealant was fitted to the thousands of components, thus achieving design reliability.

Over the years, the structure of the aircraft has proved very resistant to corrosion, not least because all water vapour is evaporated by the heated airframe during supersonic flight. Statistical studies and inspections showed that strengthening to the middle crown section of the fuselage would improve the longevity of the airframes, as would changes to certain spars and housings of the powered flying control units. Although these changes required long maintenance downtimes to incorporate, they have all been introduced. A similarly large maintenance programme was necessary to extend the working life from 6,700 to 8,500 cycles, despite the fact that the Farnborough test airframe was still intact after 21,000 thermal and mechanically induced supersonic flights.

One of the more costly problems has been the rate at which rudder and elevon control surfaces need to be changed. A series of partial in-flight failures of the honeycomb construction pointed to a need for a much-reduced time between inspections, and highlighted quality control shortcomings during the production of replacement components.

These are just some of the improvements to Concorde that have been incorporated during its operational lifetime. They show quite clearly that, where necessary, changes have been made to ensure the safety and reliability of the aircraft regardless of cost or maintenance downtime. This made the catastrophic events of July 2000 even more of a shock to the hundreds of individuals involved in flying and maintaining Concorde, not to mention the loyal and trusting passengers and supporters. The graphic images of F-BTSC streaming a high plume of flame and smoke, followed by the subsequent loss of the aircraft, highlighted the destruction of Concorde's perfect safety record. In the words of one journalist, 'the great white bird reared up as the flames bled uncontrollably from the mortally wounded aircraft', and in less than two minutes the world's only supersonic aircraft crashed into a Paris suburb.

Engineers fit some of the many hundreds of individual retaining brackets into the wing fuel tanks. (British Airways/Adrian Meredith Photography)

A new low profile radial tyre was developed for Concorde by Michelin. It is more damage-resistant and in the unlikely event of a high-speed blow-out, the casing is designed to break into small pieces that will be far less likely to damage the aircraft. (British Airways/Adrian Meredith Photography)

The flight data and sequence of events has been published in preliminary and a transcript of the report by the French *Bureau Enquêtes – Accidents* (BEA) follows below.

On Tuesday 25 July 2000 Concorde registration F-BTSC was intended to operate from Paris-Charles de Gaulle to New York-JFK airport. The flight was a non-scheduled operation, Flight Number AFR4590, on behalf of 100 German tourists en route to a cruise ship. Under the command of Captain Christian Marty were the co-pilot, flight engineer and six cabin crew members. At 14h 44 Greenwich Mean Time (GMT) (16h 44 local) the aircraft began its take-off roll on runway 26 Right. During the take-off a number of sequential problems occurred and although the aircraft became airborne it was neither able to climb above 200 feet nor accelerate beyond 200kts of airspeed. One-and-a-half minutes later the aircraft crashed into a hotel at Gonesse killing all on board.

Within a few minutes the BEA set up a team of investigators to try and discover what had happened, and most importantly to see what lessons could be applied in the future.

The inquiry process was that outlined in Annex B of the International Civil Aviation Organisation. In accordance with these provisions, the BEA invited participation from the British Air Accident Investigation Branch to join their team, supported by many experts from BAe Systems and Rolls-Royce. Observers from Germany (BFU) and America (NTSB and FAA), and regulators from France and the UK helped to complete the team, which of course included many experts from Air France, EADS and SNECMA. Representatives from British Airways and the wheel tyre manufacturers were also included.

A rear view of the Olympus engine bay with access doors open. (British Airways/Adrian Meredith Photography)

The French Ministers of Equipment, Transport and Housing set up a Commission of Inquiry which assisted the BEA in its work and which was informed periodically of progress. As required by French law, a judicial process was conducted in parallel with the accident investigation.

From the evidence available at the crash site, analysis of components on the runway and data from the various voice and data recorders, the sequence of events is clear. The flight has been broken down into three phases:

Phase 1 From the beginning of the Cockpit Voice Recorder (CVR) recording to the application of take-off power

Phase 2 From the application of take-off power to final loss of thrust on engine 1

Phase 3 Loss of control of the aircraft

PHASE 1

At the beginning of the CVR recording item 17 on the checklist (the cockpit check) was under way. The crew indicated the following data: fuel loaded 95 tons, V2 at 220 kts.

The moment of truth: Concorde G-BOAF lifts off from Heathrow on the first verification flight, 16 July 2001. (British Airways/Adrian Meredith Photography)

At 14h14 minus 04s the pre-start checklist began. The crew stated the data from flight preparation, in particular the Zero Fuel Weight (ZFW)/ Zero Fuel Centre of Gravity (ZFCG): 19.9 tonnes/52.2 per cent; the total weight of the aircraft and fuel: 186.9 tonnes and 95 tonnes; the V1, VR, V2, V2+20, and noise abatement speed: 150, 198, 220, 240, 280kts; three engine attitude: 13 degrees. The pre-start checklist ended about two minutes later. At about the same time, the crew was informed that the replacement of the thrust reversers on Engine 2 was complete.

Between 14h 17m 02s and 14h 19m 06s, the Flight Engineer (FE) began a test on the BLUE hydraulic system because of a low level on that circuit. The test was satisfactory.

At 14h 20m 06s, the Dispatcher gave the crew the final load sheet that was accepted by the Captain. Among other things, the Captain was informed of a fuel allowance of 2 tonnes for taxiing. The crew updated the take-off weight to 185.1 tonnes and corrected the ZFCG to 52.3 per cent.

At 14h 25m 54s engine start-up began. The four engines started up normally and the aircraft was authorised to taxi a few minutes later.

At 14h 37m 29s, the taxiing checklist was interrupted following the appearance of the Power Flying Control alarm. The BLUE electrical system failed and the crew decided to select the GREEN electrical system to control the rudder.

At 14h 40m 23s, the FE announced 800kg of fuel consumed during the taxiing phase, which corresponded to a take-off weight of 186 tonnes. At this weight there is no limitation related to take-off performance, and calculated parameters for V1 and VR are the same as for MTOW (185.07 tonnes). The V1 callout is effectively made 33s after powering up the engines, which corresponds to the time established during simulations at the MTOW.

At 14h 40m 37s, the pre-take-off checklist began. The transfer of fuel had modified the stated CG of 54.2 per cent during taxiing to the value of 54 per cent. The temperature of the brakes was 150 degrees celsius.

At 14h 42m 17s, the Concorde was cleared to line up and take off.

PHASE 2

At 14h 42m 30s, FDR reference time 91561, the characteristic click of the four thrust levers is heard. One second later the Captain announced take-off. A change in background noise is perceptible, a noise similar to an increase in air conditioning flow and engine speed.

The FE announced the four reheats at 14h 42m 43s and the four green lights 14 seconds later. These announcements confirm the engines were in good working order, including post combustion.

The call outs for 100kts and V1 were done at 14h 42m 55s and 14h 43m 03s. Acceleration to V1 was in exact conformity with the simulation at MTOW.

At 14h 43m 10s, a clear, short noise is heard. The speed of the aircraft was 175 kts and the distance from the runway threshold 1,722 metres. It was from that point onwards that the first parts of the water deflector, pieces of tyre and the metal strip from the DC-10 were found along the runway. A slight heading deviation to the left can then be noted at a rate estimated at 1 degree per second.

At 14h 43m 11s, a very clear change in the background noise is heard and the first tyre marks from wheel number 2 appear on the runway. The speed of the aircraft was 178kts and the distance run was 1,800 metres. The piece of tank 5 was found at this point on the runway. A large unburned kerosene stain was identified a few metres further on. Longitudinal acceleration was still normal and constant. In the following second, an incomprehensible word is heard. The speed was 182kts and the distance run was 1,885 metres. The first traces of soot appeared on the runway. The Captain began to steer to the right and almost immediately began to pull the nose up. Engine thrust and longitudinal acceleration were still normal.

At around 14h 43m 13s, minimum longitudinal acceleration was recorded and the GO LIGHTS for engines 1 and 2 went off, confirming a loss of thrust on both engines (estimated as slight for engine 1 and high for engine 2). The First Officer (FO) said 'Watch out'. (At this stage of the investigation it is not possible to explain this exclamation.) A second more significant heading deviation to the left can be noted, at a rate calculated at 2 degrees per second, probably linked to the yaw caused by the loss of thrust from engines 1 and 2. The controller told the crew that flames were visible behind the aircraft. The nose gear left the ground while a second movement of the rudder pedal is recorded to counter the yaw movement caused by the loss of thrust from engines 1 and 2. The change in the background noise heard three seconds earlier stops. The speed was 188kts and the distance run 2,090 metres.

At 14h 43m 16s, the heading deviation to the left was at its maximum when the rudder deflection reached 20 degrees, then stabilised at 10 degrees (the rudder deflection range is from −28 degrees to +28 degrees). Engine 1 recovered about 90 per cent of its nominal thrust. At the same time, the FE announced something (not understood at present). The engine 1 GO LIGHT came back on, that of engine 2 stayed off with thrust severely affected.

At 14h 43m 20s, engine 1 practically recovered its nominal thrust. The FE announced 'Failure . . . engine 2'. The announcement was logical considering the drop in N2 of over 5 per cent that confirms an engine failure (the nominal N2 at take-off is around 103 per cent). The speed was 203kts, the distance run 2,750 metres and the longitudinal pitch was +9 degrees. Engine 2's parameters were not, as expected, rising slightly.

Between times 14h 43m 18s and 14h 43m 21s, the GO LIGHTS for engines 1 then 3 and 4 went off, which is normal bearing in mind lift-off of the main landing gear shock absorber. At the end of this time period, a runway left edge light was torn out by wheel 6 of the left main landing gear. In the same time frame a selector noise is heard which has been identified as movement of the TCU from MAIN to ALTERNATE. This normal action is intended to switch the computers. A few tenths of a second later, a significant deceleration of engine 1 is identified, notably the parameters Fuel Flow: 1,323t/h, N1: 50 per cent; N2: 74.8 per cent recorded at 14h 43m 24s. A right-hand movement on the rudder pedal is also recorded.

There are indications that the significant loss of thrust on engines 1 and 2 was due to the ingestion of kerosene and/or hot gases coming from the

ignition of the leak. The slight initial loss of thrust on engine 1 would have resulted from absorption of small pieces of debris associated with the destruction of the tyre.

Lift-off occurred at 14h 43m 22s, speed 205kts, pitch +10 degrees, and the distance run 2,900 metres. In the same second, the engine 2 red fire warning came on. The associated gong is heard a little later.

At 43m 23s, engine 2's parameters are recorded with a slight failure. FF: 3,485 t/h; N1: 57 per cent; N2: 77.5 per cent.

At 14h 43m 24s, the FE announced 'shut down engine 2', and the radio altimeter indicated 25 feet. At 14h 43m 25s, the Captain asked for 'engine fire procedure'. In the same second a selector noise, which has not yet been identified, is heard. The FDR Engine Warning parameter was switched to 'de-activated' and the fire alarm stopped.

At 14h 43m 27s, the FO announced 'watch the airspeed, the airspeed, the airspeed'. Speed was then 200kts for a three-engine Vzrc with gear extended of 205kts. In the following second, a selector noise is heard which was identified as being the artificial feel selectors disengaging. A gong is also heard, identified as the alarm which follows the selector disengagement. Engine 2's N2 speed fell below 58 per cent, leading to the

Alpha Foxtrot taxies in at a rainy RAF Brize Norton on completion of the first leg of its verification flight. (Adrian Watson)

167

mode change to CONTINGENCY for engines 3 and 4. Engine 1, recovering thrust, would also change to CONTINGENCY mode seven seconds later. (The thrust provided would then be equal to an engine at full thrust with reheat with CONTINGENCY.) At the same time, 14h 43m 28s, engine 2 was no longer being supplied with fuel and its N1 and N2 parameters are characteristic of a wind milling engine.

At 14h 43m 29s, a selector noise identified as a fire handle is heard. (NB: the engine 2 fire handle was found in the pulled position in the wreckage.)

At 14h 43m 30s, the Captain called for the gear to be retracted. Speed was 200kts, the radio altimeter indicated 100 feet and the calculated climb rate was +750ft/min. In the following seconds the controller confirmed to the crew that there were strong flames behind the aircraft and the FE repeated 'the gear'. The alarm indicating detection of smoke in the toilets is heard. (This alarm has not yet been explained.)

At 14h 43m 35s, the FE repeated for the FO 'the gear (Jean)'. Engine 1 was running normally. In the following second a gong is heard. This was most likely the alarm indicating low oil pressure due to the shutdown of engine 2.

At 14h 43m 37s, the FE repeated 'the gear', the FO answered 'no'. It is very likely that the red WHEEL light, situated next to the gear retraction controls, was illuminated by detecting the reduced pressure of the tyre destroyed on wheel 2. In this case, the procedure requires that the landing gear should not be retracted.

At 14h 43m 39s, the Captain ordered 'gear retract' and three seconds later the engine 2 fire alarm was reactivated with its associated gong. It stopped a few seconds after the FE fired the extinguisher bottles. At 14h 43m 45s, the FE stated 'I'm firing it'. (NB: the two extinguishers situated in the left wing were found fired off in the wreckage.) At the same time, the Captain asked '(are you) shutting down engine 2 there?' and the FE answered 'I've shut it down'.

At 14h 43m 49s, the FO said 'the airspeed'. The speed was then about 200kts. This warning is repeated again about ten seconds later. The first differences between the plane's attitude and the pilot's actions on the flight controls begin to appear, differences which could be explained by damage to the left wing caused by the fire, in particular at the level of the left inner elevon. The angle of attack was then 13 degrees.

At 14h 43m 56s, the FO stated 'the gear isn't retracting'. This non-retraction of the landing gear has yet to be explained. There are two possible explanations for this:

the loss of the GREEN hydraulic system which commands the retraction of the landing gear (although no gong associated with this loss is heard); one of the conditions for retraction of the gear (gear alignment) is possibly not met.

At 14h 43m 58s, the engine 2 fire alarm sounded for the third time and continued to sound until the end of the flight. In the following second the GPWS 'Whoop, Whoop, Pull Up' is heard three times. This is in accordance with mode 3 of GPWS.

At 14h 44m, a first disturbance of engine 1's FF and P7 parameters is noted. A second disturbance is recorded eight seconds later. At the same time the rudder switched to mechanical mode, which led to the loss of the yaw auto-stabilisation function. Roll/pitch and fore-and-aft control/tilt interactions are noted, which might confirm the loss of effectiveness of the left inner elevon.

At 14h 44m 12s, engine 1's parameters show a clear deceleration. This seems to result from the ingestion of kerosene and hot gases produced by the fire and internal damage caused by ingestions at take-off. Only engines 3 and 4 were still running.

PHASE 3

In the following twenty seconds, the angle of attack would vary over twelve seconds from 12 degrees to a value above 25 degrees, left roll would pass from 2.13 degrees to 113 degrees (a value recorded 4 seconds before the end of the recording), and the heading would vary from 270 degrees to 115 degrees. The significant loss of thrust from engines 3 and 4 is recorded five seconds before the end of the recording, probably due to distortion of the air entering the intakes, the angle of attack being above 25 degrees and the left roll close to 100 degrees.

In these extreme conditions, no detailed examination was carried out on the loss of control leading to the impact, which was probably due to the combination of lateral asymmetry, significant thrust/drag imbalance and structural damage caused by the fire. In fact, since the aircraft had exceeded the angle of attack and roll values approached during the certification tests, there is no data available which would allow its behaviour in such conditions to be described.

The aircraft and hotel were destroyed on impact. The initial reaction was shock and disbelief but the vivid video recordings removed all doubt. Air France and British Airways cancelled flights for that day, although Air France subsequently made this a permanent grounding, pending the result of the accident investigation. British Airways resumed flying but then ceased when the initial recommendation convinced the authorities that 'the Certificates of Airworthiness of Concorde should be suspended until appropriate measures had been taken to ensure a satisfactory level of safety as far as the tyre destruction-based risk is concerned'.

Media coverage was almost unprecedented: the failure of a twentieth-century technological icon, the hitherto unblemished safety record, the tremendous sadness in the German town of Mönchengladbach, from where most of the passengers had travelled, all combined to make this the lead news item for several days. Graphic pictures taken by amateur and professional photographers were also unique and were shown time and time again. The disaster was taken into the lives and homes of millions around the world. Accident inquiry teams always work under a cloud of sadness and pressure to discover why, but in this case the pressures were immensely higher.

Gradually, as some of the facts became clear, other information was debated and would eventually need answers. But at the interim stage of the investigation, in the opinion of the BEA nothing appeared to have emerged to contradict the following scenario.

On take-off from runway 26 Right and at a speed of 175kts, the Concorde ran over a metal strip from a DC-10 which had taken off several minutes earlier. This strip pierced the tyre on wheel 2 of the left landing gear. One or more pieces of tyre were thrown against the lower surface of the wing at the level of tank 5. This led to the rupture of this tank in the process (which will be studied for some time to discover any further implications on all aircraft) which seemed to combine the deformation of the tank wall with the propagation of a fluid wave linked to the displacement of the kerosene. A major leak resulted. The leaking kerosene was agitated in the turbulence from the landing gear and ignited. The causes of this ignition are also being studied. Engines 1 and 2 were then severely disrupted by the hot gases resulting from the ignition of the leaking kerosene. The aircraft took off trailing a very large stabilised flame which caused structural damage throughout the flight. The fire alarm for engine 2 triggered and the crew carried out the engine fire procedure. Engine 1 recovered to almost normal thrust. The aircraft was flying slowly and remained at low altitude when the crew noted that the landing gear would not retract due to the left door not opening. This was owing to the damage caused either by the impacts resulting from the destruction of the tyre or by the flames. The crew mentioned a possible landing at the Le Bourget landing strip. A loss of thrust in engine 1 occurred a few seconds later as a result of the ingestion of a mixture of hot gases/kerosene and internal damage caused by the ingestion of structural debris. The angle of attack and roll of the aircraft then increased sharply and control of the aircraft was lost due to the combination of the thrust dissymmetry, the severe thrust-drag imbalance and perhaps the structural damage due to the fire. The thrust from the engines 3 and 4 suddenly reduced, probably due to a voluntary reduction associated with the distortion in the air stream. The aircraft crashed.

Manufacturers, regulators and airlines therefore had a relatively clear task, regardless of other factors. The fuel in the main tanks had to be protected from debris and particularly from the effects of a disintegrating tyre. Furthermore, there were significant benefits to be gained from the production of a more damage-resistant tyre and the reduction in the number of ignition sources in the undercarriage area.

The sense of purpose and the magnitude of the problems quickly produced the team spirit and cooperation that had produced Concorde in the first place. Anglo-French inter-governmental teams were formed under which investigative and design teams searched for solutions. A multitude of options was considered and evaluated, many were discarded while others were vigorously pursued.

The preferred solutions, which emerged, were:

• Reinforce the vulnerable fuel tanks with rubber/Kevlar linings
• Change the tyre design to a lower profile, radial tyre
• Reinforce electrical wiring in the undercarriage bay
• Demonstrate that the engines can function with an ingress of fuel and foreign objects

As the work to progress these requirements got under way, meetings took place within and between the prime manufacturers of the airframe,

electronics and engines industries. There was also continuous consultation with regulators, government departments and the airlines to ensure a consistency of views and eventual consensus on the proposed solutions.

The media interest continued but gradually began to fall off, removing some of the associated pressures. Other interested parties such as national and private research facilities became involved.

Meanwhile, other questions and information about the accident arose. Some were dealt with quickly, but others will require explanation at some point in the future. The 'what ifs?' will continue, possibly long after the aircraft is back in the sky, but the effects of these points and their inter-relationships may never be fully established. Others will be shown to have had no material impact on the incident whatsoever.

Some of these points include:

• Why was a large spacer missing from the undercarriage and what effect, if any, did this have?
• What condition was the tyre before it left the ramp?
• What fuel was on board at the point of departure from the gate and at the threshold?
• How was this fuel distributed and which values and pumps were used?
• Why were 19 bags not included in the take-off weight and the centre of gravity calculations, and did this have any relevance?
• What was the actual centre of gravity on take-off, and if it was beyond the aft limit had this been done before?
• What was the actual take-off weight?
• What were the actual wind, temperature and pressure on take-off and the maximum take-off weight associated with these conditions? If the actual take-off weight exceeded the performance limit, why did the crew continue?

The Phoenix rises: four BA Concordes fly the flag 'somewhere over Great Britain'. (British Airways/Adrian Meredith Photography)

- Was the rate of acceleration down the runway normal?
- Why did the aircraft veer initially to the left?
- Why was the piece of metal that had fallen from the Continental DC-10 not detected?
- Would a less worn tyre have been more damage tolerant?
- What was the puncture method of the fuel tank, and had there been any previous stresses or damage to the tank?
- What ignited the fuel-air mixture?
- Why did the aircraft veer even further left and why was full rudder not applied?
- The aircraft was rated 11kts before the calculated VR. Was this because the aircraft would have left the paved surface?
- What multiple warnings persuaded the Flight Engineer to close down No. 2 engine at 25ft rather than the normal 400ft and what impact might this have had?
- Why were engines 1 and 2 showing fluctuating power?
- How quickly was the fire destroying components, systems and flying characteristics?
- What was happening to the in-flight movement of the centre of gravity?
- What finally caused the aircraft to lift and crash?

Whatever answers are available in the future, there is no doubt that the lessons will be learnt and wherever relevant applied to other aircraft. What will not be possible will be to replicate the sheer complexity of thought in the minds of the passengers, cabin crew and in particular the flight crew. The latter would be receiving a multitude of major systems warnings and failures, the aircraft would be manoeuvring in a completely different way to anything they could have possibly experienced, and everything would be happening at an alarming pace. No one who has ever flown Concorde can possibly say how he would have reacted in such a situation.

Once again, the question was asked: 'Should Concorde fly again?' As on all previous occasions, those who asked the question were hoping for a negative answer and had either not done their research, did not fully understand the implications of cancellation, or had some other agenda. And once again, Concorde champions were needed. The most influential and informed turned out to be Rod Eddington, the new Chief Executive of British Airways. He appeared determined to take Concorde back into service, provided it could be done safely and with the complete confidence of engineers, crew, manufacturers and regulatory authorities.

Meetings were arranged, technical options evaluated further, and provisional test programmes were drafted just as they had been thirty years before. The likely cost of all the work was hard to forecast, so it was put to one side, but Concorde would fly again almost regardless of cost. As it turned out, the actual figure was close to the original guesses and fully justifiable in a business plan.

The most time-consuming task was the design, manufacture and fitting of the Kevlar fuel tank linings. Thousands of separate, different brackets were needed to fix the lining to the inside of the fuel tanks. Each Concorde is slightly different so many small modifications were needed. The

engineers who fitted each piece into the tanks worked many long hours in difficult physical conditions, but with the same pride and dedication that has always made the Concorde project special.

Manufacturers and regulators also played a massive role. This was another ground-breaking task that required ground-tests on engines and intakes, and taxiing trials at low and high speeds. Air France flew to a test base at Istres on a number of occasions, while British Airways consulted on a verification flight programme. Part-way through the programme, Michelin realised that they could produce a lower profile radial tyre for Concorde. This tyre would be significantly more damage resistant and weigh less than the tyres currently in use. Furthermore if damaged, any significant tyre disintegration that resulted in breakaway pieces would be much smaller than with the existing cross-ply profile, thereby causing considerably less damage to wing or undercarriage.

This development proved to be viable and new radial tyres were delivered in time for verification flights. This breakthrough added to the level of confidence in the aircraft, and meant that the Certificate of Airworthiness could be renewed with the full agreement of all concerned. It also meant that passengers could feel even more reassured that safety was paramount.

Keeping the dream alive: Captain Mike Bannister, the late Brian Trubshaw, and Captain Jock Lowe. (Studio B10)

Other systems were deemed to need modification to ensure complete compliance with Regulatory requirements, but these were relatively small when compared to the fuel tank and tyre changes and they were all completed by the summer of 2001. Meanwhile, the interiors of the British Airways Concordes were redesigned with new seats, interior décor, galleys and toilets. Unlike the re-certification work, this refurbishment project was set up as a turnkey, fixed-price contract and it, too, was delivered on time in midsummer 2001.

The day that all those involved had been waiting for arrived on 16 July 2001. Concorde G-BOAF took off from London on a full supersonic verification flight followed by a landing at a wet and windy RAF Brize Norton in Oxfordshire. The flight was a complete success and demonstrated not only the correct functioning of all the systems and modifications, but also that the overall weight increase was acceptable. The extra weight of the Kevlar, and a slight increase in unusable fuel, were offset by the reduced weights of the cabin interiors and new tyres. The residual increase in all-up weight of approximately 300kg was of no operational significance. After a further flight and much analysis and paperwork, the evidence was submitted to the Regulators on 15 August 2001. Some further, minor work was deemed necessary but on 6 September the next milestone was reached – the Certificate of Airworthiness was restored. The dream could begin again.

On that day, Brian Trubshaw would have started writing this chapter and he would have been prouder than anyone. He knew he had been central in producing a unique and wonderful aircraft that had entered the dreams and lives of millions. He would have taken just as much pleasure in seeing his aircraft return to commercial service in 2001 as he had done for its first entry into commercial service in 1976.

Concorde has a special place in the hearts of all who fly, operate or simply watch the aircraft. We can confidently expect it to continue fulfilling these expectations for many years to come.

APPENDIX I:
ANGLO-FRENCH
AGREEMENT

LONDON, 29 NOVEMBER 1962

The Government of the United Kingdom of Great Britain and Northern Ireland and the Government of the French Republic.

Having decided to develop and produce jointly a civil supersonic transport aircraft; have agreed as follows:

Article 1

(1) The principle of this collaboration shall be equal sharing between the two countries, on the basis of equal responsibility for the project as a whole, of the work, of the expenditure income by the two Governments, and of the proceeds of sales.

(2) This principle, which shall be observed as strictly possible, shall apply, as regards both development and production (including spares), to the project considered as a whole (airframe, engine, system and equipment).

(3) The sharing shall be based upon the expenditure corresponding to the work carried out in each country, excluding taxes to be specified by agreement between the two Governments. Such expenditure shall be calculated from the data of the present agreements.

Article 2

The two Goverments having taken note of the agreement dated 25 October 1962 between Sud Aviation and the British Aircraft Corporation (BAC) and of the agreement dated 28 November 1961, between Bristol Siddeley and the Société Nationale d'Étude et de Construction de Moteurs d'Aviation (SNECMA) have approved them with provisions, which are the subject of agreement between Governments.

Article 3

(1) The technical proposals, which shall form the basis for the joint undertaking by Sud Aviation and BAC, comprise a medium range and a long range version of the aircraft.

(2) The Bristol Siddeley – SNECMA BS/593/ turbojet engine shall be developed jointly for the aircraft by Bristol Siddeley on the British side and by SNECMA on the French side.

Article 4

In order to carry out the project, integrated organisations of the airframe and engine firms shall be set up.

Article 5

A Standing Committee of officials from the two countries shall supervise the progress of the work, report to the Governments and propose the necessary measures to ensure the carrying out of the programme.

Article 6

Every effort shall be made to ensure that the programme is carried out, both for the airframe and for the engine, with equal attention to the medium range and the long-range versions. It shall be for the two integrated organisations of the British and French firms to make detailed proposals for the carrying out of the programme.

Article 7

The present Agreement shall enter into force on the date of its signature. In witness whereof by their respective Governments, having signed the present Agreement. Done in duplicate at London, this 29th day of November 1962 in the English and French languages, both texts being equally authoritative. For the Government of the United Kingdom of Great Britain and Northern Ireland:

JULIAN AMERY
PETER THOMAS

For the Government of the French Republic:

[G. DE COURCEL]

APPENDIX II:
CONCORDE
DEVELOPMENT

Aerodynamic Improvements

| | | c_L | LIFT/DRAG RATIO | | CL/CD |
			Aircraft A	Aircraft B	GAIN
TAKE OFF	Zero Climb Gradient	0.77	3.94	4.24	7.6
	Second Segment	0.614	4.97	5.58	12.3
	Noise abatement procedure	0.28	6.00	7.38	23.0
APPROACH		0.6	4.35	4.75	9.2
HOLD AT 250 KTS. 10.000 FT.		0.28	9.27	13.1	41.3
SUBSONIC CRUISE AT M = 0.93		0.2	11.47	12.92	12.6
SUPERSONIC CRUISE ISA + 5°C	610 ENGINE	0.125	7.14		7.7%
	610 ENGINE + 25%	0.152		7.69	

Aircraft `A` **Aircraft `B`**

Supersonic

Droop
Leading Edge

Take-off ~ Hold

Subsonic cruise ~ Approach ~ Landing

APPENDIX III: CONCORDE DETAILS

WEIGHTS – MAX PERMISSIBLE

Start of taxi	186,880kg	(412,000lb)
Start of take-off	185,070kg	(408,000lb)
Landing	111,130kg	(245,000lb)
Weight without fuel	92,080kg	(203,000lb)

DIMENSIONS

Length	202ft 4in	(61.66m)
Span	83ft 10in	(25.6m)
Height of fin	40ft 2in	(12.2m)

Notes

1 Maximum weight for the start of take-off from any American airfield is 182,250kg (404,600lb) for environmental reasons.
2 Fuel-saving landings may be made up to 130,000kgs under increased landing weight procedure.
3 BA use kilograms. AF uses pounds.

APPENDIX IV:
US CLEARANCE OF CONCORDE

US CLEARANCE FOR CONCORDE

US Secretary of Transportation, Mr. William Coleman, issued the following decision on Wednesday, 4th February, 1976.

THE DECISION

"After careful deliberation, I have decided for the reasons set forth below, to permit British Airways and Air France to conduct limited scheduled commercial flights into the United States for a trial period not to exceed 16 months (Footnote 5/) under limitations and restrictions set forth below. I am thus directing the Federal Aviation Administrator, subject to any additional requirements he would impose, for safety reasons or other concerns within his jurisdiction, to order provisional amendment of the operations specifications of British Airways and Air France, to permit those carriers, for a period of no longer than 16 months from the commencement of commercial service, to conduct up to two Concorde flights per day into JFK by each carrier, and one Concorde flight per day into Dulles by each carrier. (Footnote 6/) These amendments may be revoked at any time upon four months' notice, or immediately in the event of an emergency deemed harmful to the health, welfare or safety of the American people. The following additional terms and conditions shall also apply:

1. *No flight may be scheduled for landing or take-off in the United States before 7 a.m. local time or after 10 p.m. local time.*
2. *Except where weather or other temporary emergency conditions dictate otherwise, the flights of British Airways must originate from Heathrow Airport and those of Air France must originate from Charles De Gaulle Airport. (Footnote 7/)*
3. *Authorization of any commercial flights in addition to those specifically permitted by this action, shall constitute a new major federal action within the terms of NEPA and therefore require a new environmental impact statement.(Footnote 8/)*
4. *In accordance with FAA regulations (14 CFR S91.55), the Concorde may not fly at supersonic speed over the United States or any of its territories.*
5. *The FAA is authorised to impose such additional noise abatement procedures as are safe, technologically feasible, economically justified, and necessary to minimize the noise impact, including, but not limited to, the thrust cut-back on departure.*

I am also directing the FAA, subject to Office of Management and Budget clearance and Congressional authorization, to proceed with a proposed high-altitude pollution program (HAPP), to produce the data base necessary for the development of national and international regulation of aircraft operations in the stratosphere.

I herewith order the FAA to set up monitoring systems at JFK and Dulles to measure noise and emission levels and to report the result thereof to the Secretary of Transportation on a monthly basis. These reports will be made public within 10 days of receipt.

I shall also request the President to instruct the Secretary of State to enter into immediate negotiations with France and Great Britain so that an agreement that will establish a monitoring system for measuring ozone levels in the stratosphere can be concluded among the three countries within three months. The data obtained from such monitoring shall be made public at least every six months. I shall also request the Secretary of State to initiate discussions through ICAO and the World Meteorological Organization on the development of international stratospheric standards for the SST.

Footnotes

5/ The 16 months will enable 12 months of data collection (during all four seasons) and four months of analysis.

6/ The FAA is the proprietor of Dulles and it is therefore part of my decision today to direct the Federal Aviation Administrator to permit one Concorde flight per day at Dulles by each carrier under the conditions noted. The situation with respect to JFK may be complicated by the fact that under Federal policy that has hitherto prevailed, a local airport proprietor has had authority under certain circumstances to refuse landing rights. If for any legitimate and legally binding reason, it should turn out that the JFK part of the demonstration could not go forward —— and no one has indicated to me any such final disposition by JFK's proprietor —— that would obviously be extremely unfortunate and would greatly diminish, but in my opinion it would not destroy, the validity of the demonstration.

7/ As will appear, one reason this demonstration is being permitted, despite the environmental problems discussed herein, is to avoid discrimination against foreign manufacturers and carriers. I surely see no reason why we should treat the Concorde better than it is treated at home. Thus, I am not about to subject those who live near JFK and Dulles to noise, however slight the increment, that the British and French Governments regard as too great for the neighbors of Heathrow and Charles De Gaulle.

8/ It is not contemplated that another EIS would be required to permit continuation, beyond 16 months, of the six flights for which provisional permission is now being granted. It is most definitely contemplated —— indeed, that is the whole point of today's decision —— that the Secretary of Transportation, in deciding whether to permit continuation of the six flights, will give serious attention to the various data collected during the first twelve months, and assembled and analyzed during the demonstration's final four months, and approach the question of continuation of permission for the six flights beyond the 16th month, without any presumption either way being created by today's decision. The data and analysis will be made public".

APPENDIX V: CONCORDE CHRONOLOGY

1959	March	STAC report recommends UK develop long-range supersonic transport.
1962	November	Angle-French Agreement signed.
1963	June	Pan American, BOAC and Air France sign Concorde 'options'. Medium-range version enlarged.
	October	Labour Government announces it will review programme.
1965	January	Government announces review complete, programme to continue despite financial and economic doubts.
	May	Preproduction design announced. Preproduction design revised. Options reach a total of seventy-four from sixteen airlines.
	December	Prototype 001 rolled out at Toulouse.
1968	February	Government announces £125m production loan.
	September	002 rolled out at Bristol; production design revised.
1969	March	First flight of 001.
	April	First flight of 002.
1970	December	Design changes made.
1972	April	Production of sixteen aircraft made.
	July	BOAC orders five Concordes, Air France (AF) orders four.
	December	Government increases production loan to £350m. Design changes made.
1974	January	Pan American and TWA drop Concorde options.
	July	Wilson and Giscard d'Estaing agree to complete only sixteen Concordes.
1975	March	Draft US environmental impact statement published.
	November	Final US environmental impact statement published.
1976	January	Concorde airline service begins to Bahrain and Rio de Janeiro. Coleman hearing on Concorde US services.
	February	Coleman decision approves Washington services.
	March	Port Authority of NY and NJ bans Concorde from Kennedy Airport.
	May	Washington service begins.

1977	**May**	New York litigations begins with Concorde 1 case.
	September	Concorde 2 case appeal confirms port authority ban unlawful.
	October	US Supreme Court denies port authority appeal.
	November	New York services begin.
1978	**June**	Adams confirms Coleman approval, exempts Concorde from noise rules.
1979	**February**	BA to write off Concorde purchase cost.
	September	Unsold Concordes to go to Air France and British Airways.
1981	**April**	Commons Trade and Industry Committee report says project 'had acquired a life of its own and was out of control'.
	October	Future of Concorde discussed by UK and French ministers.
1982	**February**	Trade and Industry Committee report reaffirms criticism.
	October	AF drops Washington service.
1984	**March**	BA takes over support costs from British Government. AF takes over support costs from French government.
1994	**November**	BA drops Washington service.
1999	**September**	BA and AF continue scheduled services and charters.
2000	**July**	AF Concorde F-BTSC crashes at Paris with loss of all on board. AF and BA Concorde fleets grounded pending outcome of accident investigation.
2001	**September**	C of A restored.
	October	BA resumes Concorde scheduled services.

BAC's Concorde production line at Filton with Concorde 212 (G-BOAE) in the foreground. (BAe Systems)

APPENDIX VI: CONCORDE ANTI-STALL SYSTEMS

An anti-high angle of attack system is fitted that consists of angle of attack trim (automatic trimming of elevons as angle of attack increases) which is part of the auto-stabilisation system set at 11° and above and a stick shaker which activates at 16°. This is signalled from either of the two Air Data Computers (ADC) and operates on the captain's control column but it is also felt on the co-pilot's column through mechanical linkage. An anti-stall system augments the basic pitch auto-stabilisation with a super-stabilisation junction creating an unmistakable warning through the artificial feel system and becoming active above above 13.5°.

Two anti-stall systems are provided with No. 1 system having priority. The super-stabilisation system applies down elevon deflection limited to 8°. This is done by the pitch auto-stabilisation channel depending on angle of attack, pitch rate and airspeed declaration. At 19° a stick wobbler is introduced causing both control columns to pulsate by modulating pressure in the artificial feel jacks against any manual nose up stick force. The wobbler contains a phase advance up to 3°. At speeds below 140k the super-stabilisation commands a simultaneous 4° down elevon. This is a delicate solution compared to the rather crude stick pushers with all their inherent dangers.

APPENDIX VII: CONCORDE FLYING HOURS

BRITISH AIRWAYS

Manufacturer's No.	Civil Registration	Total Hours
206	G-BOAA	21,900.29
208	G-BOAB	21,236.57
204	G-BOAC	21,959.54
210	G-BOAD	21,607.52
212	G-BOAE	21,737.06
216	G-BOAF	16,517.36
214	G-BOAG	14,385.06

AIR FRANCE

Manufacturer's No.	Civil Registration	Total Hours
203	F-BTSC	11,413.11
205	F-BVFA	16,337.34
207	F-BVFB	12,850.18
209	F-BVFC	12,500.12
211	Out of Service	5,821.08
213	F-BTSD	11,788.48
215	F-BVFF	11,442.55

Notes

1   Air France figures quoted in July 1999 are hours at October 1998.
2   Air France Concordes average approximately 500 hours per annum.
3   BA hours are at 31 August 1999.
4   Air France 211/F-BVFD grounded 1982 and scrapped 1994.
5   Air France 203/F-BTSC crashed near Paris on 25 July 2000 with the loss of all on board.

APPENDIX VIII:
TESTIMONY OF
WILLIAM
MAGRUDER

BAC/Aérospatiale Flight News published Bill Magruder's testimony, made on 4 January 1976.

The safety of Concorde as seen by an American SST expert.

During the Concorde public hearings in Washington DC on 5th January, Mr William M. Magruder, Executive Vice-President, Piedmont Aviation and former Director of the US SST Development Office, testified on the subject of Concorde.

Part of his statement concerned the safety aspects of the Franco-British airliner which is recorded in the official transcript published by the US Department of Transportation.

Eighty per cent of all the incidents and accidents in civil air transport happen at low speeds and close to the ground. The Concorde wing is extraordinary in this area.

Almost all operational low-speed safety margins, certified by Administrator McLucas's FAA people are determined on the basis of a thing called the aerodynamic stall. The stall occurs when the air flow of the wing ceases to flow smoothly, separates as the airplane falls. Close to the ground this can be catastrophic. Our margins on present-day jets close to the ground are as low as 10 to 15 knots on take-off.

Present-day jets, and I have certified many models of them, flown by almost every one in the Free World, including most of the supersonic airplanes, use lift-spoiling spoilers for lateral control, further reducing the stall margins on take-off and approach. They have wing flaps that, if improperly retracted, can reduce the entire safety margin to zero and this has happened. They have trimmable stabilizers which, if improperly set for take-off or landing, can prevent the airplane from taking off or cause a stall.

The Concorde wing design removes every single one of those safety hazards, without exception. Furthermore, it does not have an aerodynamic stall.

When people talk about these noise abatement maneuvers, the Concorde design has twice the maneuver margin of any subsonic jet flying today close to the ground and around the airport during take-off and landing.

During landing, this particular design has a ground cushion that virtually makes the landing flare automatic, increasing accuracy as well as safety.

The moveable nose was invented in this country on the Lockheed design, as a result of the most extensive operational tests ever done. These tests clearly showed in the University of California fog chamber that the Concorde, which adopted the new moveable design of the US, as did the 'Concordksi', that that airplane will be able to see twice as many approach lights at 100 feet and a quarter-mile visibility, as any of the subsonic jets. That is a tremendous addition to safety for bad weather approach.

On approach, we were worried about vortices from preceding airplanes, gusts, maneuvers, and unusual characteristics, such as improper spoiler extension or wing flap extension. The Concorde can sustain twice as much gust or maneuver margin as any airplane flying today in commercial aviation.

It is my opinion, after 30 years of flight testing, designing and engineering airplanes, that this could be the safest commercial airline ever built. I do not think that the travelling public should be denied that potential. Now, at high speed, the subsonic jets had a thing called the jet-upset problem. It was so serious that one of your predecessors almost grounded the entire jet fleet in 1961. I was on that investigation board with Secretary Alan Boyd. This is a situation where an airplane that gets going too fast results in the pilot reporting that they cannot get the nose up and they cannot level the wings. It has not happened just once; it has happened hundreds of time. Some airplanes have lost some engines. Some airplanes have lost 35,000 feet in these dives. It comes from the type of tail and the wing design of the subsonic jets. At slightly over the design speed, the longitudinal control is so marginal that test pilots cannot quickly recover from a dive. If they are in a bank and they exceed a certain Mach number, then when the pilot uses the rudder to raise the wing, which is normal, the bank could steepen. Corcorde has none of these characteristics, so even in a high-speed area, it is a very safe airplane.

Fuel reserves have come up. I have been a pilot most of my life. Two things require large fuel reserves, the long time from take-off to landing, during which winds can act on you; this airplane cuts the time in half.

Most important, at the altitudes Concordes fly, winds seldom if ever exceed 20 knots. When your speed is 1,350 miles an hour, there is no effect on an SST from wind. For the first time in aviation history, civil travelers can count on no-wind flights every time they go. That means less fuel reserve impacts and better safety, reliability, meeting connecting flights, etcetera.

This could be the safest airplane ever built. The Concorde is the first commercial airplane in my 30 years of experience that has not had a serious incident during the flight test program and it has flown more than three times the test flights of anything ever done with jets in this country. This is quite a safety tribute.

GLOSSARY OF TERMS AND ABBREVIATIONS

A&AEE	Aircraft & Armament Experimental Establishment
ADC	Air Data Computer
AFCS	Automatic Flight Control System
ARB	Air Registration Board
ATC	Air Traffic Control
AVS	Air Ventilated Suit
BA	British Airways
BAe	British Aerospace
BAC	British Aircraft Corporation
BOAC	British Overseas Airways Corporation
Boundary layer	The layer of air extending from the surface of the object to the point where no dragging effect is discernible.
CA	Controller of Aircraft
CAA	Civil Aviation Authority
C of A	Certificate of Airworthiness
CAD	Commercial Aircraft Division
CAT III	Low visibility conditions
CEAT	French government establishment
CEV	Centre D'essais en Vol
CG envelope	Centre of gravity
Delcon	Inertial navigation used by BA
DTI	Department of Trade and Industry
Elevons	Flight control surfaces combining elevator and aileron
ETPS	Empire Test Pilot's School
FAA	Federal Aviation Agency
FTG	Flight Test Group
GTS	Gas Turbine Starter

HF	High Frequency radio signals
IATA	International Air Transport Agency
ILS	Instrument Landing System
Kelvin	Measurement of temperature
L/D	Lift/Drag ratio
Litton	Inertial navigation system used by Air France
LP	Low Pressure compressor or turbine
Lv	Lateral stability
M=1.0	Speed of sound
MEPU	Term for auxiliary power unit
Mmo	Max permitted Mach number
MRCA	Multi Role Combat Aircraft (Tornado)
NACA	Forerunner of NASA
NASA	National Aeronautics and Space Administration
NPL	National Physical Laboratory
N1/N2	Engine speed relationship
PFCU	Power Flight Control Unit
PNYA	Port of New York and New Jersey Authority
Psi	Cabin pressure limit
RAE	Royal Aircraft Establishment
SATCO	Senior Air Traffic Control Officer
SETP	Society of Experimental Test Pilots
SNECMA	Société Nationale d'Étude et de Construction de Moteurs d'Aviation
SST	Supersonic Transport
STAC	Supersonic Transport Advisory Committee
TRA	Thrust-reverser After
TSS	Transport Supersonic Standards
TWA	Transworld Airlines
USAF	United States Air Force
VMCA	Minimum control speed in the air after engine failure
Vmo	Maximum permitted airspeed
VTT	Target threshold speed
VZRC	Zero rate of climb speed
WAT	Weight, Altitude, Temperature

INDEX